RAND NATIONAL DEFENSE RESEARCH INSTITUTE

Critical Materials

Present Danger to U.S. Manufacturing

RICHARD SILBERGLITT, JAMES T. BARTIS,
BRIAN G. CHOW, DAVID L. AN, KYLE BRADY

Prepared for the National Intelligence Council
Approved for public release; distribution unlimited

The research described in this report was prepared for the National Intelligence Council. The research was conducted within the RAND National Defense Research Institute, a federally funded research and development center sponsored by the Office of the Secretary of Defense, the Joint Staff, the Unified Combatant Commands, the Navy, the Marine Corps, the defense agencies, and the defense Intelligence Community under Contract W74V8H-06-C-0002.

Library of Congress Cataloging-in-Publication Data is available for this publication.

ISBN: 978-0-8330-7883-4

The RAND Corporation is a nonprofit institution that helps improve policy and decisionmaking through research and analysis. RAND's publications do not necessarily reflect the opinions of its research clients and sponsors.

RAND® is a registered trademark.

Published 2013 by the RAND Corporation
1776 Main Street, P.O. Box 2138, Santa Monica, CA 90407-2138
1200 South Hayes Street, Arlington, VA 22202-5050
4570 Fifth Avenue, Suite 600, Pittsburgh, PA 15213-2665
RAND URL: http://www.rand.org/
To order RAND documents or to obtain additional information, contact
Distribution Services: Telephone: (310) 451-7002;
Fax: (310) 451-6915; Email: order@rand.org

Preface

This report describes the results of a study of the sources and reliability of the supply of imported materials on which United States manufacturers are dependent. It should be of interest to a broad spectrum of individuals and organizations in the materials and manufacturing sectors as well as government, private sector, and non-profit organizations involved with or concerned about those sectors.

This research was sponsored by the National Intelligence Council and conducted within the Intelligence Policy Center of the RAND National Defense Research Institute, a federally funded research and development center sponsored by the Office of the Secretary of Defense, the Joint Staff, the Unified Combatant Commands, the Navy, the Marine Corps, the defense agencies, and the defense Intelligence Community.

For more information on the RAND Intelligence Policy Center, see http://www.rand.org/nsrd/ndri/centers/intel.html or contact the director (contact information is provided on the web page).

Contents

Figures

Tables

Summary

Critical Materials: The Problem

The U.S. economy, and especially its manufacturing sector, is dependent on the supply of raw and semi-finished materials used to make products. While the United States has extensive mineral resources and is a leading global materials producer, a high percentage of many materials critical to U.S. manufacturing are imported, sometimes from a country that has the dominant share of a material's global production and export. In this situation, U.S. manufacturers are vulnerable to export restrictions that limit their access to these materials and that can result in two-tier pricing, under which domestic manufacturers in the producing country have access to materials at lower prices than those charged for exports, thereby hindering the international competitiveness of U.S. manufacturers and creating pressure to move manufacturing away from the U.S. and into the producing country.

Several reports over the past four years have analyzed the economic importance and supply risks of a large number of materials from various perspectives, with substantial overlap and agreement. Starting from this base, we focus our analysis on a subset of materials for which production is concentrated in one or a few countries and for which the following conditions apply:

- The dominant producer is outside the United States.
- The United States has appreciable net imports.
- The dominant producers have shortfalls in their quality of governance, as measured by the Worldwide Governance Indicators (WGI) published by the World Bank.

We find that one country, China, is in a unique position in that it is the only country that satisfies the above conditions and produces more than 50 percent of the global production of more than one material critical to U.S. manufacturing. In fact, China produces more than 50 percent of 11 of these materials, nine of which were identified in one or more of the previous reports as having high economic importance and high supply risk (see Figure S.1).

Three of these materials (rare earths [REs], antimony, and tungsten) are difficult to substitute without significantly increasing the cost or decreasing the performance of the products they are used to make. REs are used in lasers and many components of electronic devices and defense systems, antimony is critical to flame retardant plastics and textiles, and tungsten is used to produce cemented carbides for cutting tools used in many industries. Moreover, the United States is heavily dependent on imports for all three of these materials; virtually 100 percent of REs and 90 percent of antimony are imported.

Trends in China's Role

China's market share of the global production of critical materials has grown dramatically over the past two decades from a strong position to an overwhelmingly dominant one. For example, China's share of tungsten and antimony production, already 60 percent in 1990, is now over 80 percent for tungsten and about 90 percent for antimony. As China's market share and domestic consumption have grown, its mate-

Figure S.1
Percentage of Global Production (Mining) of Key Materials Within a Single Country

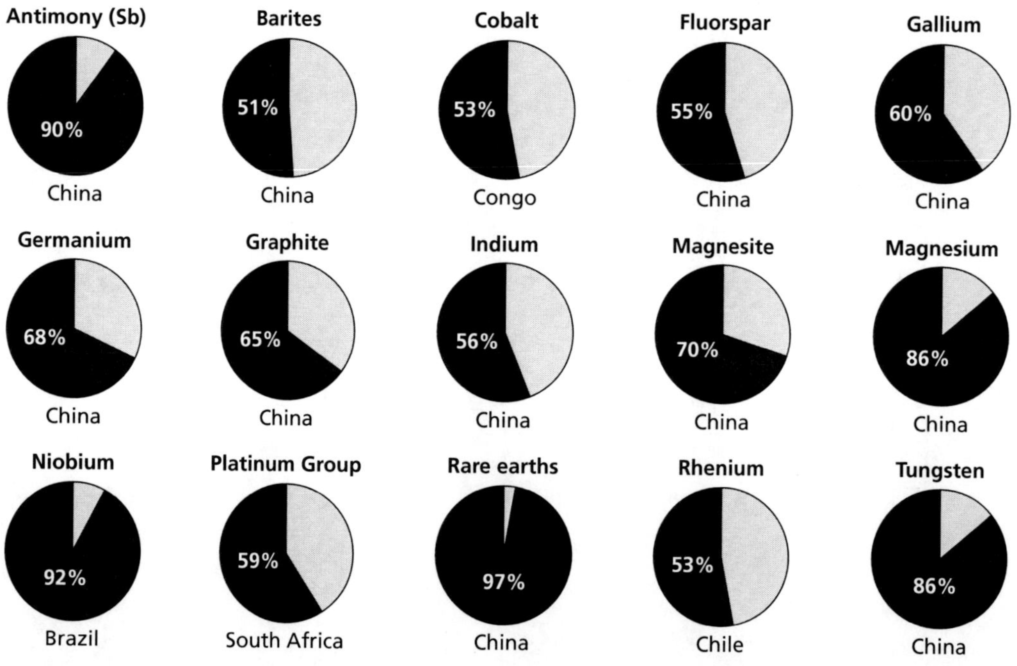

SOURCE: U.S. Geological Survey, *Minerals Commodity Summaries*, Pittsburgh, Penn.: U.S. Government Printing Office, 2012; International Organizing Committee for the World Mining Congresses, *World Mining Data*, Vol. 26, 2011.

RAND *RR133-S.1*

rials export policies have moved in a direction that has created concern among its customers. In particular, China has instituted a combination of production controls, export restrictions (e.g., quotas and tariffs; see Figure S.2), mine closings, and company consolidation.

The increases in export restrictions illustrated in Figure S.2 initially focused almost solely on REs and tungsten, but in 2007 and 2008 broadened to include other materials. The combined effect of export restrictions and worldwide demand for these materials has contributed to significant increases in their price and, in some cases, volatility on the world market. For example, the price of rare earth metals doubled from 2010 to 2011, while prices of some elements, such as lanthanum and cerium (both REs), reportedly rose as much as 900 percent. Prices of antimony and tungsten more than doubled over this same period.

The export restrictions have resulted in a two-tier pricing system for certain materials of which China is the dominant producer, including its rare earth metals, allowing China's domestic manufacturers to pay a lower price than the export price. By undercutting the market price, China's actions have both discouraged the continuation of manufacturing in the United States and provided motivation for moving U.S. manufacturing operations specifically to China.

Figure S.2
Concurrent Rise in China's Market Share of Key Materials and the Number of Export Restrictions Applying to Them

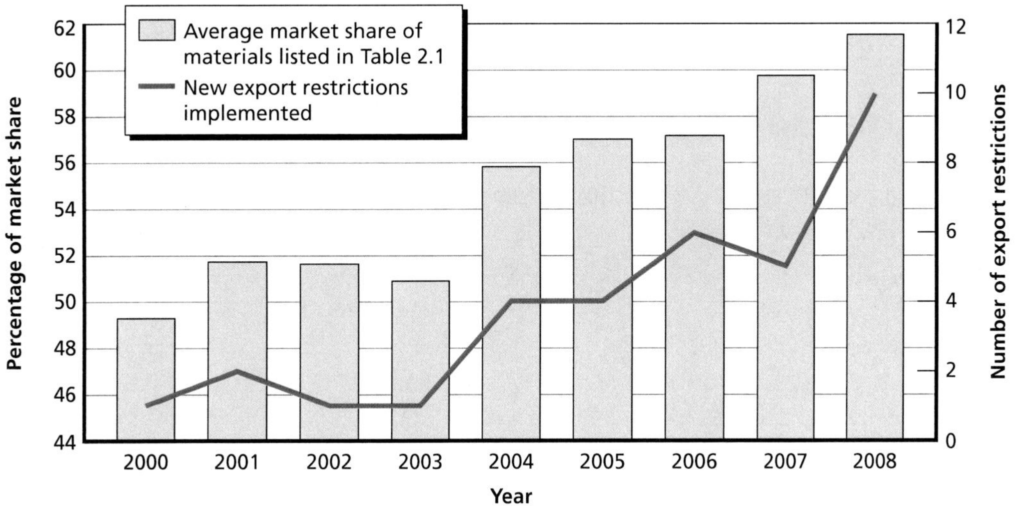

SOURCES: U.S. Geological Survey, *Minerals Commodity Summaries*, 2003–2010; Jane Korinek and Jeonghoi Kim, "Export Restrictions on Strategic Raw Materials and Their Impact on Trade and the Global Supply," *OECD Trade Policy Papers*, No. 95, Paris: OECD Publishing, 2010; Strategic Metal Investments, Ltd., *China's Growing Role in the Production and Supply of Minor Metals: Part II*, May 10, 2010.
RAND *RR133-S.2*

Attempts to Counter China's Actions

In response to these actions, two separate complaints were brought against China at the World Trade Organization (WTO) over the past three years. In 2009, the United States, followed by the European Union (EU), and later Mexico, brought a complaint against China's trade restrictions on various forms of bauxite, coke, fluorspar, magnesium, manganese, silicon carbide, silicon metal, yellow phosphorus, and zinc. The WTO ruled in 2011 that China's export duties and export quotas on these materials were in violation of WTO rules. This ruling was upheld after appeal in January 2012 and, at the time of this writing, China's compliance actions were not yet defined. In March 2012, the United States, EU, and Japan brought a new WTO complaint against China's trade restrictions on REs, tungsten, and molybdenum. At the heart of both of these complaints, as stated by U.S. and European trade representatives, are China's export restrictions, leading to the two-tier pricing structure and its effect on the competitiveness of U.S. and European firms.

As evidenced by the dates given in the previous paragraph, actions at the WTO can take several years. Opening new mines outside China, including the necessary permitting and compliance with regulations and standards, can also take several years and can require hundreds of millions, or even billions, of dollars in a market that is uncertain because of the market power held by a dominant producer. Yet the impacts on manufacturers dependent on imported materials occur much more rapidly. A 2011 global survey of manufacturers[1] found that a majority believe that supply risks will rise significantly over the next decade and that the impact will be felt throughout the supply chain. In some industries (renewable energy, automotive, and energy and utilities), responses suggested that supply instability is currently being experienced.

A Case Study: Tungsten

As an example, we studied the supply situation for tungsten, a critical raw material and one for which U.S. manufacturers depend on imports. China is the controlling producer of tungsten, with more than 80 percent of 2010 world production and estimated 2011 world production. The leading use of tungsten today is for cemented carbides, composite materials that are used worldwide for drilling, cutting, and machining. These materials are critical to every industrial application that involves cutting or component wear—mining; construction; oil and gas exploration; tools and dies; and the cutting of wood, plastics, and metals. Tungsten is thus a basic commodity underpinning the global manufacturing sector.

---

1 Price Waterhouse Coopers, *Minerals and Metals Scarcity in Manufacturing: The Ticking Timebomb: Sustainable Materials Management*, December 2011.

We found that China is the dominant exporter of both raw tungsten and the intermediate tungsten products that are essential inputs to manufacturing. As a result of China's export policies and growing domestic demand for tungsten, analysts both inside and outside of China project a tight supply situation to continue for the next several years. The lack of access to tungsten materials by manufacturers outside of China presents a threat to the manufacturing sector elsewhere in the world and creates pressure on manufacturers to move operations to China. U.S. manufacturers have responded to this threat by increasing secondary production from waste and scrap, reducing their dependence on imports by about one-third. They are also taking steps to reduce the amount of tungsten used in products and to find alternative materials. However, it is not clear how much more secondary production can be increased, and reduction and substitution measures that do not affect product performance require concerted effort. In the meantime, difficult access to supply increases pressure to move manufacturing from the United States to China. Moreover, prolonged disruption in the supply chain for tungsten and other critical raw materials could jeopardize the U.S. science and technology base for these materials and, consequently, U.S. innovation and competitiveness in new products manufactured from them.

Conclusion: Concentration of Supply and Effective Response

We conclude from the data and analyses described in the text of this report that the critical issues associated with the supply of minerals are less about the minerals themselves than they are about where the raw and semi-finished materials that are derived from these minerals and that underpin economies are produced and processed. One clear conclusion is that countries commanding a large market share of a material's production can distort mineral commodity markets through production controls and export restrictions. Thus it is the concentration of supply, in particular the concentration among producing countries that either have weak governance or that control production at the governmental level, or both, that can increase the potential for supply disruptions.

China is the dominant producer and exporter of many critical materials. Its strategic material policies include (1) trying to gain control of production outside of China (i.e., by obtaining controlling interests in mines outside of China that produce materials such as antimony and REs, of which it is already an overwhelmingly controlling producer) and (2) establishing production quotas and export restrictions. These policies have contributed to large price increases, some price volatility, and tight markets, as well as uncertainty that can hinder the financing of new mining projects. Moreover, China's policies contrast with those of other countries with high market shares, such as Chile (with 53 percent of rhenium) and Australia (with 51 percent of zirconium), which do not implement export restrictions, instead allowing market forces to largely determine the supply and demand of the minerals they produce.

The impact of these policies on the global manufacturing sector suggests the need for two types of actions: (1) those that can increase resiliency to supply disruptions or market distortions and (2) those that can provide early warning of developing problems resulting from the concentration of production. Actions to increase resiliency should be aimed at the diversification of production and processing, as well as the development of new methods of extraction, processing, and manufacturing that will improve the efficiency of material use and increase the recovery of materials from waste and scrap. Actions to provide early warning could be based on benchmarking market activity with diversified commodity markets and international coordination and cooperation that could potentially prevent the situation from reaching the level requiring action at the WTO. The goal of such coordination and cooperation should be to smooth market distortions while allowing for the natural economic development of producing countries.

Acknowledgments

We gratefully acknowledge helpful discussions and interactions with many colleagues, including Steven Berner, Cortez Cooper, John Fei, Eric Landree, Victoria Greenfield, John Parachini, Andrew Scobell, Howard Shatz, Jeffrey Stricker, Lloyd Thrall, and Kathi Webb of RAND, as well as staff of the U.S. Departments of Energy and Homeland Security, the U.S. Environmental Protection Agency, the U.S. Geological Survey, and the U.S. Trade Representative. We also profited from discussions with several individuals in the private sector who are directly involved with materials and manufacturing, as well as discussions with staff of the National Mining Association and the International Tungsten Industry Association. We thank all of these individuals for providing information and perspectives that contributed greatly to our research.

We are especially grateful to the peer reviewers of this report, Andrew Scobell and Howard Shatz of RAND, and Professor Rod Eggert of the Colorado School of Mines. Their insightful comments and suggestions led to substantial improvements in the quality of the manuscript.

Abbreviations

APT	ammonium paratungstate
DOE	Department of Energy
EC	European Commission
EU	European Union
FOB	Free on Board
HHI	Herfindahl-Hirschman Index
IDA	Institute for Defense Analysis
ITIA	International Tungsten Industry Association
mtu	metric ton unit
NDS	National Defense Stockpile
NRC	National Research Council
PGM	Platinum group metals
RE	rare earth element
REACT	Rare Earth Alternatives in Critical Technologies
SMSP	Strategic Materials Security Program
USGS	U.S. Geological Survey
VAT	value-added tax
WGI	Worldwide Governance Indicators
WTO	World Trade Organization

CHAPTER ONE

Introduction

The U.S. economy, especially its manufacturing sector, is dependent upon the supply of raw and semi-finished materials[1] used to make products. While the United States has extensive mineral resources and is a leading global materials producer, a high percentage of many materials critical to U.S. manufacturing are imported.[2] This report is concerned with the reliability of such imports and the potential for uncertainty and disruption in the supply chain through which U.S. manufacturers obtain critical raw and semi-finished materials, which are defined for the purposes of this report as materials that are essential inputs to manufacturing operations. Our key concern is that the lack of access to such materials, principally due to export restrictions imposed by a country with an overwhelming share of production, leads to two-tier pricing, under which domestic manufacturers in the producing country obtain the materials at lower prices, as well as hinders the international competitiveness of U.S. manufacturers and creates pressure to move manufacturing from the U.S. to the producing country.

A further issue with supply disruption is that the U.S. science and technology base that supports manufactured products was built on and depends on the presence of U.S. manufacturers producing these products from raw and semi-finished materials. Prolonged disruption in the supply of raw and semi-finished materials required by these manufacturers could put the science and technology base in jeopardy, which would further reduce U.S. innovation capability and competitiveness in the development of new, higher-performance products.

Early in our study, it became evident that a small number of mineral-producing nations are responsible for a very large share of the global production of certain economically important materials. Moreover, we observed sharp price increases for many of the materials of which China is the preeminent producer. For these reasons, we

---

1 By raw materials, we mean ores and their concentrates produced by physical processing to increase the percentage of the desired materials in the mined ore. By semi-finished materials, we mean materials produced by chemical processing of ores and concentrates, including intermediate products for further processing, as well as powders and formed materials such as sheets, wires, and bars.

2 For a comprehensive list of import percentages, see U.S. Geological Survey, *Minerals Commodity Summaries*, Pittsburgh, Penn.: U.S. Government Printing Office, 1996–2012.

decided to focus our efforts on China by reviewing its role as a controlling producer of several critical materials and by taking a detailed look at tungsten as a case example.

As we approached completion of our study, the United States, Japan, and the European Union (EU) announced that they were filing complaints with the World Trade Organization (WTO) against China's trade restrictions on rare earth elements (REs), tungsten, and molybdenum.[3] This set of complaints mirrors and expands upon a 2009 complaint by the United States and the EU against China's trade restrictions on various forms of bauxite, coke, fluorspar, magnesium, manganese, silicon carbide, silicon metal, yellow phosphorus, and zinc.[4] At the heart of these complaints is China's two-tier pricing structure and its effect on the competitiveness of U.S. and European firms.

Recent Analyses of Critical Raw Materials

While the reliability of material supplies has long been of concern, the topic of critical raw materials has gained urgency with the growth of U.S. dependence on foreign suppliers in recent years. Four recent studies, summarized below, provided the backdrop and starting point for this RAND work.

In 2008, the National Research Council (NRC) Committee on Critical Mineral Impacts on the U.S. Economy developed a matrix framework for assessing the criticality of a given mineral based on estimates of the economic impact of restriction on its supply and the likelihood of such restriction. This NRC committee applied its framework to nine materials and two families of materials, including metals used in electronics and high-temperature alloys, REs used in electronics and energy and defense systems, and platinum group metals (PGMs) used in catalysts in the automotive and chemical industries.[5] They concluded that three of the nine materials and both families of materials were in the matrix quadrant with the highest economic impact and highest supply risk, namely PGMs, REs, manganese, indium, and niobium.[6]

---

3 See World Trade Organization, *China—Measures Related to the Exportation of Rare Earths, Tungsten and Molybdenum*, Dispute Settlements: DS431, DS432, DS433, September 24, 2012b, c, d.

4 See World Trade Organization, *China—Measures Related to the Exportation of Various Raw Materials*, Dispute Settlement: DS394, February 22, 2012.

5 The materials and families of materials considered were: copper, gallium, indium, lithium, manganese, niobium, PGMs (platinum, palladium, rhodium, iridium, osmium, ruthenium), REs (lanthanum, cerium, praseodymium, neodymium, promethium, samarium, europium, gadolinium, terbium, dysprosium, holmium, erbium, thulium, ytterbium, lutetium), tantalum, titanium, and vanadium.

6 Committee on Critical Mineral Impacts of the U.S. Economy, Committee on Earth Resources, and the National Research Council, *Minerals, Critical Minerals, and the U.S. Economy*, Washington, D.C.: National Academies Press, 2008, p. 165.

The U.S. Department of Energy (DOE) adapted the NRC matrix by substituting importance to clean energy for impact on the economy. This study analyzed the supply situation of 16 materials, including nine of the REs, that it judged critical to current and future energy systems such as wind energy, electric and hybrid vehicles, and high-efficiency lighting.[7] The study concluded that, over the short term (present–2015) and medium term (2015–2025), five REs (dysprosium, europium, terbium, yttrium, and neodymium) were in the matrix quadrant with the highest importance to clean energy and the highest supply risk. For the short term, dysprosium, europium, and terbium have the highest importance and highest supply risk. Dysprosium and terbium continue to be rated as having the highest supply risk in the medium term.[8]

The Institute for Defense Analysis (IDA) assessed the likely availability of materials needed for defense systems using a set of defense planning scenarios, including wartime, and estimated that, under these planning scenarios, the United States would face shortfalls in 21 of the 51 materials assessed. For 18 of these materials, shortfalls exceeded the September 2009 capacity of the National Defense Stockpile (NDS), namely aluminum oxide, antimony, bauxite (the ore from which aluminum is produced), beryl ore,[9] bismuth, cobalt, fluorspar (the source of hydrofluoric acid, used extensively in the chemicals industry), manganese, niobium,[10] silicon carbide, tantalum, tin, gallium, germanium, rhenium, rhodium, ruthenium, and yttrium.[11]

In 2010, a study group sponsored by the European Commission (EC) assessed the supply risk for 41 critical raw materials, which included essentially all of the materials covered in the previously discussed reports. The study group concluded that 14 of these materials were of concern to the EU because of their combined high supply risk and high economic importance, including antimony, beryllium, cobalt, fluorspar, gallium, germanium, graphite, indium, magnesium, niobium, PGMs, REs, tantalum, and tungsten.[12]

---

[7] The DOE analyzed the supply situation for lanthanum, cerium, praseodymium, neodymium, samarium, europium, terbium, dysprosium, yttrium, lithium, indium, gallium, tellurium, manganese, cobalt, and nickel. The DOE considered yttrium an RE element.

[8] U.S. Department of Energy, *Critical Materials Strategy*, December 2011, p. 4.

[9] "Dollar valuation of beryl ore shortage is zero to two decimal places" (James S. Thomason, Robert J. Atwell, Ylli Bajraktari, James P. Bell, D. Sean Barnett, Nicholas S.J. Karvonides, Michael F. Niles, Eleanor L. Schwartz, *From National Defense Stockpile (NDS) to Strategic Materials Security Program (SMSP) Vol. I: Evidence and Analytic Support*, Alexandria, Va.: Institute for Defense Analyses, 2010, pp. 10–11).

[10] Listed in the IDA report as columbium, which was the former name of this element.

[11] Thomason et al., 2010.

[12] European Commission, "Critical Raw Materials for the EU," *Report of the Ad-hoc Working Group on defining raw materials*, June 2010, p. 6.

Our Approach

Although each organization had a different perspective, there is great overlap and agreement in their reports on the importance and supply risk of certain materials. Using the set of materials studied in these reports as a starting point, we analyzed the extent to which the production of these important materials is controlled by one or a few nations and how that control can create uncertainty or disruption in supply. In Chapter Two, we consider the reliability of supply of the 41 critical raw materials analyzed in the EC study.[13] Our objective is to identify the extent to which the production of these materials is concentrated in countries for which concern about the reliability of supply is raised by governance issues, such as political instability, government control of material production, or restrictions on exports. To measure the concentration of production, we use the Herfindahl-Hirschman Index, designed to measure the concentration of market power and international trade. As a measure of the quality of governance, we use the Worldwide Governance Indicators (WGI) for 2010. As described on the World Bank web site, the WGI project provides percentile indicators for 213 economies over the period of 1996–2010 for six dimensions of governance: Voice and Accountability; Political Stability and Absence of Violence; Government Effectiveness; Regulatory Quality; Rule of Law; and Control of Corruption.[14] For each of these dimensions, a higher percentile represents better governance. We use the average of the six percentile indicators as a metric of governance, with 100 being the best and zero the worst. Chapter Three analyzes the current and potential effects the concentration of production has on the reliability of the supply of critical raw and semi-finished materials. The chapter also reviews strategies for mitigating these effects. Chapter Four presents the case study of tungsten, an important raw material for the production of tungsten carbide cutting tools, widely used in oil and gas drilling, mining, and manufacturing, as well as for the production of alloys and electrical components. Chapter Five presents our conclusions and discusses possible response options to supply restrictions.

---

13 We used the EC study as our starting point because it provided data on the production, trade, and commercial and peacetime use of the largest number of materials.

14 The World Bank, *Worldwide Governance Indicators*, 2012. The WGI are described in Daniel Kaufmann, Aart Kraay, and Massimo Mastruzzi, *The Worldwide Governance Indicators: Methodology and Analytical Issues*, World Bank Policy Research Working Paper 5430, September 2010.

CHAPTER TWO

Concentration of Production of Critical Raw Materials

The most commonly used measure of concentration in commodity markets is an index attributed to the economists O. C. Herfindahl and Albert O. Hirschman.[1] For our purposes, the Herfindahl-Hirschman Index (HHI) is defined as the sum of the squares of the fraction of market share controlled by the 50 largest entities producing a particular product. If 50 countries are active in producing a specific commodity and each has the same market share, the index would be 0.02, which is very close to its lower limit of zero. The maximum value of the index is unity, which corresponds to a single country being responsible for 100 percent of the production of a commodity.[2]

The U.S. Department of Justice and the Federal Trade Commission use the HHI to examine antitrust issues involving corporate mergers. According to guidelines established by the U.S. Department of Justice, an HHI of between 0.15 and 0.25 signals a "moderately concentrated" market, and an HHI above 0.25 indicates a "highly concentrated market." Under these guidelines and the definition of the HHI, whenever a single firm has a market share of over 50 percent, the market would be considered highly concentrated. A market can also be highly concentrated when multiple firms hold appreciable shares of the market. For example, if three firms each control 30 percent of a market, the HHI is at least 0.27. Likewise, whenever a single firm controls more than 38.7 percent of a market, the market is considered moderately concentrated. Another example of a moderately concentrated market would be one with three firms that each control 23 percent of the market.[3]

Figure 2.1 shows the HHI for the 41 EC critical raw materials that were analyzed in the EC study. Here, market shares are based on mine production. Extending the

---

1 For historical background on the creation of the HHI, see Albert O. Hirschman, "The Paternity of an Index," *American Economic Review*, Vol. 54, No. 5, September 1964, p. 761.

2 Some users (for example, the U.S. Department of Justice) calculate the HHI using percentages of market share, as opposed to fractional shares, which are decimals that range between 0 and 1. Using percentages creates an index that has a maximum value of 10,000. The two methods yield equivalent results, being linearly related by a factor of 10,000.

3 See "Herfindahl-Hirschman Index," U.S. Department of Justice, undated. For example, an HHI of 0.2 (center of the moderately concentrated range) would result from five countries with equal shares of production.

Figure 2.1
HHI Index for the 41 EC Critical Raw Materials

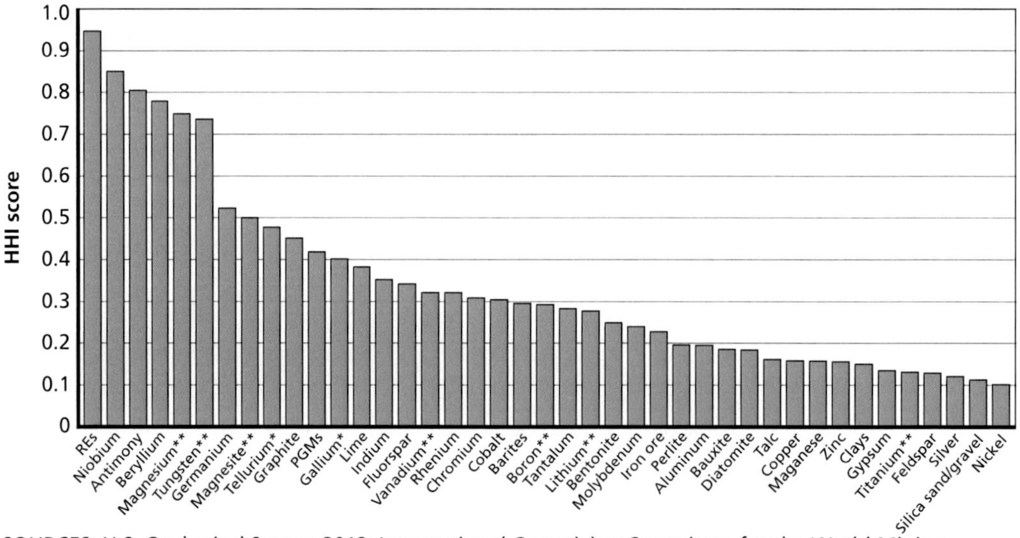

SOURCES: U.S. Geological Survey, 2012; International Organizing Committee for the World Mining Congresses, 2011.
*Most recent production data from 2009.
**Excludes U.S. production, which is not disclosed by USGS to protect proprietary data.
RAND *RR133-2.1*

Justice Department's guidelines for market concentration from firms to nations, the production of 24 of these 41 materials would qualify as highly concentrated, and the production of an additional 11 of these materials would qualify as moderately concentrated. While the extension of these guidelines from firms to nations would be exact only if all nations exercised government control over their producing firms, it is consistent with our focus on nations with weak governance, or which control production. In both instances, there is the strong potential for export restrictions or supply disruptions to affect all producers within a country, in which case the government is a surrogate for a company in that it controls the availability of materials to the rest of the world.

We now further focus our analysis on those materials that not only have concentrated production, but also meet the following three criteria:

1. The dominant producer is outside the United States.
2. The United States has appreciable net imports.
3. The dominant producers have shortfalls in their quality of governance.

To implement the first criterion, we subtract the U.S. market share from the HHI so that the adjusted HHI will measure the concentration of non-U.S. production. This will significantly reduce the HHI of materials for which the U.S. is a major producer, e.g., beryllium. For the second criterion, we eliminate those materials for which net imports represent less than 10 percent of U.S. consumption. This criterion removes one substance, namely lime, from the EC list of 41 critical raw materials. To address the third criterion, we use the average of the six 2010 WGI to measure quality of governance. We then define an *adjusted HHI* according to the following formula:

$$\text{Adjusted HHI} = \sum (100\text{-average WGI})\text{x}(\text{market share})^2,$$

where the sum is over all producing countries except the United States, and average WGI denotes the average of the six WGI percentile indicators described in the previous chapter.

This adjusted HHI, shown in Figure 2.2, ranges from zero to 100, where 100 would correspond to a single country producing 100 percent of the world's supply of a material and having all six WGI indicators in the 0th percentile. Our rationale for this adjustment of the HHI is to produce an index for which an increase represents not only the increasing concentration of production (as for the HHI), but also the increasing concentration of production by producers with low quality of governance, as indicated by low WGI percentiles. The multiplication of the market shares by 100 minus the average of the WGI percentiles has the effect of increasing the unadjusted HHI, but the increase is greater for countries with low WGI percentiles and less for countries with high WGI percentiles. For example, since Australia's average WGI percentile is 92, its market shares are multiplied by eight, whereas China's average WGI percentile

Figure 2.2
HHI (Minus U.S. Production) Adjusted for Foreign Supplier Governance

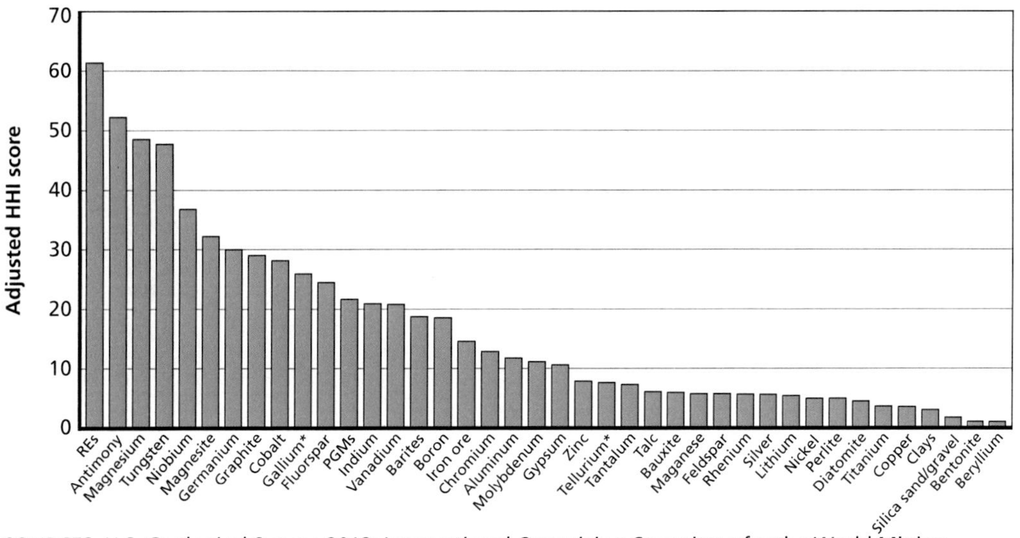

SOURCES: U.S. Geological Survey, 2012; International Organizing Committee for the World Mining Congresses, 2011.
*Most recent production data from 2009.
RAND *RR133-2.2*

is 35, so its market shares are multiplied by 65, an order of magnitude more. Thus the adjusted HHI strongly emphasizes producing countries with low WGI percentiles.

There are 16 materials and families of materials for which this adjusted HHI is above 15, which would correspond, for example, to an unadjusted HHI of .25 (our threshold for highly concentrated) and an average WGI percentile of 40 percent (higher than that of China, but lower than that of Brazil and South Africa, which are both approximately 60 percent). Twelve of these materials with high production concentrations were identified as being highly important and having a high supply risk by one or more of the reports cited in Chapter One: REs, antimony, magnesium, tungsten, niobium, germanium, graphite, cobalt, gallium, fluorspar, PGMs, and indium.

Appendix A lists the top three producers of all 41 EC critical raw materials. A small number of countries dominate this list: China, the United States, Australia, Russia, South Africa, Brazil, and Chile. However, only six countries produce more than 50 percent of any material, a level of market control equivalent to unadjusted HHI of greater than .25, or, according to our definition, a highly concentrated market: China, the United States, South Africa, Brazil, Chile, and Congo. Moreover, China's position is unique, as it produces more than 50 percent of 12 of the 41 EC critical raw materials, 9 of which were identified as having high importance and high supply risk by one or more of the reports cited in Chapter One. By contrast, each of the other countries produces more than 50 percent of only one of the 41 EC critical raw materials.

China's unique position is further illustrated by Table 2.1, which shows the percentages of 2010 world production, the HHI, 100 minus the WGI percentile, and the adjusted HHI for 13 materials and two families of materials with the highest adjusted HHI scores. Of the nine materials for which a single country has the highest share of global production, only one, niobium, is produced outside of China. For the remaining eight, China is responsible for at least 60 percent of global production and, in some cases, much more, including 97 percent of REs, 90 percent of antimony, and 86 percent of magnesium and tungsten. As we describe in Chapter Three, China's export policies with respect to these critical materials have led to serious concerns among nations whose manufacturers are dependent upon imports of these materials from China.

Of these materials, three (REs, antimony, and tungsten) are materials that are difficult to substitute without significantly increasing the cost or decreasing the performance of the products they are used to make. For example, REs are used as catalysts for petroleum processing and automotive emissions reduction, for permanent magnets, phosphors, lasers, and many components of electronic devices and energy and defense systems.[4] Antimony is critical to flame retardant plastics and textiles.[5] Tungsten is used to produce cemented carbides for cutting tools used widely throughout U.S.

[4] See, for example, Thomas G. Goonan, *Rare Earth Elements–End Use and Recyclability*, U.S. Geological Survey, Pittsburgh, Penn.: U.S. Government Printing Office, 2011.

[5] U.S. Geological Survey, 2012.

Table 2.1
Key Indicators of the Security of Supply for Important Raw Materials

Country	Material	Market Share (%)	HHI	100 Minus the WGI Percentile	Adjusted HHI
China				65	
	Rare earths	97	.95		62
	Antimony (Sb)	90	.81		52
	Tungsten (W)	86	.74		48
	Magnesium	86	.75		49
	Magnesite	70	.50		32
	Germanium	68	.53		30
	Graphite	65	.45		29
	Gallium	60	.40		26
	Indium	56	.36		21
	Fluorspar	55	.35		22
	Barites	51	.30		19
	Vanadium	39	.32		19
Brazil				43	
	Niobium	92	.85		37
Russia				74	
	Platinum Group	28	.42		21
	Vanadium	26	.32		19
Congo				84	
	Cobalt	53	.31		28
South Africa				41	
	Platinum Group	59	.42		21
	Chromium	46	.31		12
	Vanadium	33	.32		19
Chile				16	
	Rhenium	53	.32		6
	Lithium	37	.29		5
	Copper	34	.16		3

SOURCE: U.S. Geological Survey, 2012; International Organizing Committee for the World Mining Congresses, 2011.

industries.[6] Moreover, the United States is heavily dependent upon imports of all three materials, and virtually 100 percent of REs and antimony are imported.[7]

---

6 British Geological Society, *Tungsten*, 2011.

7 U.S. dependence on tungsten imports was above 60 percent for decades, although in the past year this dependence was reduced to less than 40 percent through secondary production in the United States from recycled or recovered material.

CHAPTER THREE

China's Role as a Controlling Producer

China's unique role as the dominant producer of so many important raw materials has emerged as a consequence of three factors:

- China's large resource base, due to its size and geographic location.
- The Chinese government's long-term emphasis on mineral production, including substantial investment in mining and processing.
- China's ability to produce raw materials at lower cost than many other producers because of its relatively lax environmental and occupational health and safety standards and regulations.

Because of their inability to compete with China's low-price exports of raw materials, many mines and processing plants outside of China have closed in recent years.[1] Over the past two decades, this has led to China's dramatic rise from its previously strong position to its current dominant position in global raw material production, as illustrated in Figure 3.1.

China's Policies Cause Concern Among Its Customers

Until fairly recently, China was viewed as a reliable, low-cost supplier of raw materials. However, as China's market share and domestic consumption have grown, changes to its material export policies have created concern among its customers. In particular, a combination of production controls, export restrictions (e.g., quotas and tariffs), mine closings, and company consolidation[2] has contributed to significant price increases and, in some cases, volatility on the world market. Figure 3.2 illustrates how China's

1 For example, the U.S. Geological Survey (2012) reported that REs and antimony were not mined in the United States in 2011 and that only one U.S. mine produced tungsten.

2 See, for example, Jeonghoi Kim, "Recent Trends in Export Restrictions," *OECD Trade Policy Papers*, No. 101, Paris: OECD Publishing, 2010.

Figure 3.1
Growth of China's Global Raw Material Production

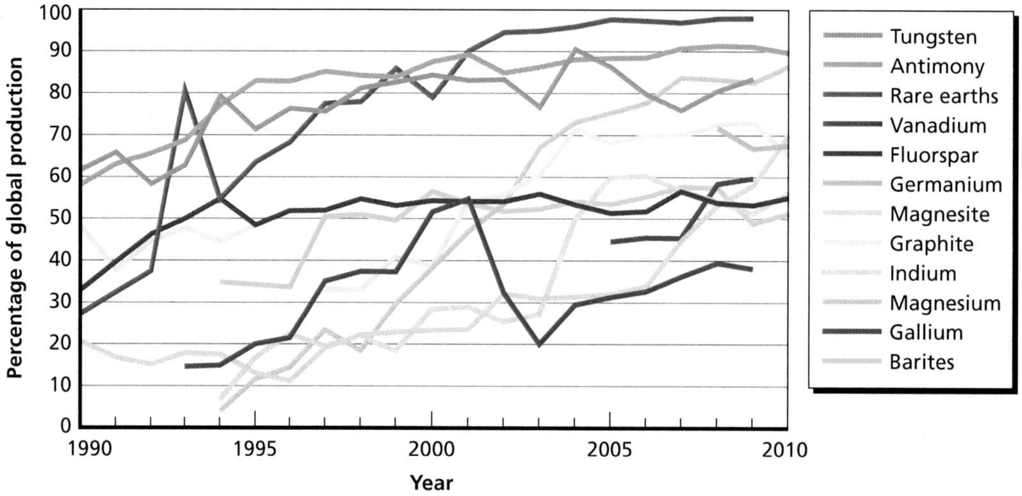

SOURCES: U.S. Geological Survey, 1996–2011; International Organizing Committee for the World Mining Congresses, 2011.
NOTE: Data unavailable on Chinese market share for germanium prior to 2008. Gallium data are from International Organizing Committee for the World Mining Congresses, 2011.
RAND *RR133-3.1*

level of export restrictions has risen along with its market share for the materials shown in Table 2.1 and Figure 3.1.[3]

The left-hand scale in Figure 3.2 shows China's average market share for these materials, while the right-hand scale shows the total number of export restrictions placed on these materials per year. In addition to export quotas and tariffs, these restrictions have included the reduction or elimination of value-added tax (VAT) rebates, export bans on waste and scrap, and directed actions, such as a limit on the export of molybdenum to the EU from August 2001 through February 2002 following the EU's imposition of dumping duties and export rules (including licenses) for specific materials that require customers to be selected or approved. These restrictions have been applied differently to different forms of materials, such as ore and concentrate, oxide, and metal. A detailed analysis of the market effects of these restrictions for specific materials is beyond the scope of this report. The simple count shown in Figure 3.2 merely indicates the increase in export-restriction activity concurrent with the increase in Chinese market share. These increases in export restrictions initially focused almost solely on REs and tungsten, but broadened in 2007 and 2008 to include antimony,

---

[3] Figure 3.2 is similar to a chart that appears in Strategic Metal Investments, Ltd., 2010. The data can be found in Korinek and Kim, 2010.

Figure 3.2
Chinese Export Restrictions and Market Share

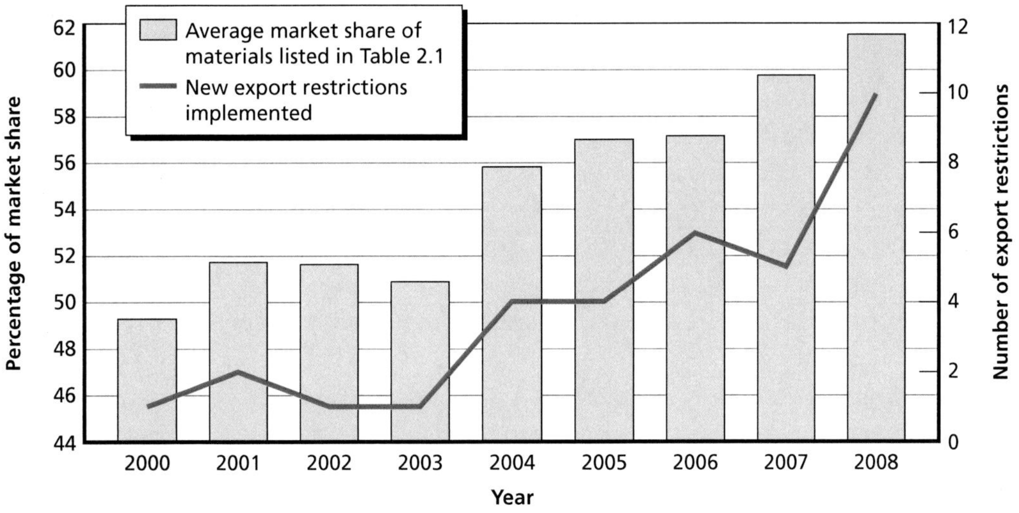

SOURCES: U.S. Geological Survey, *Minerals Commodity Summaries*, 2003–2010; Jane Korinek and Jeonghoi Kim, 2010; Strategic Metal Investments, Ltd., 2010.
NOTE: Market share data is displayed here as China's share of total world production, calculated individually for each raw material in Table 2.1 and Figure 3.1, and averaged. Export restriction data represents the total number of new policy barriers to export (in the form of quota decreases, VAT rebate cancellations, licensing requirements, etc.) that were enacted during each year.
RAND *RR133-3.2*

germanium, and indium.[4] The combined effects of these export restrictions and the worldwide demand for these materials has contributed to significant price increases and, in some cases, volatility on the world market. For example, the price of RE metals doubled from 2010 to 2011, and the prices of some elements, such as lanthanum and cerium (both REs) were reported as rising as much as 900 percent.[5] Prices then dropped sharply in the latter part of 2011, although still remaining above 2010 levels. Prices of antimony and tungsten more than doubled over this same period.[6]

China's export restrictions have had major ramifications for global manufacturing trends. For example, because of export tariffs and price increases stemming from export restrictions, China can provide its domestic manufacturers with raw materials at lower prices than those charged on the world market. As described in the WTO

[4] Reductions in export quotas for tungsten are discussed in Chapter Four.

[5] K. A. Gshneider, Jr., "The Rare Earth Crisis—The Supply/Demand Situation for 2010–2015," *Material Matters*, Vol. 6, No. 2, 2011, p. 32.

[6] Michael Montgomery, "Tungsten Price Pushes to Historic Highs," *Tungsten Investing News*, February 23, 2011a; for antimony price data see United States Antimony Corporation, home page, 2012.

complaints referenced in Chapter One, this has resulted in significant negative effects on the competitiveness of non-Chinese manufacturers and created pressure to move manufacturing plants to China from other countries. Table 3.1 demonstrates this issue by showing prices for various RE elements in the fourth quarter of 2011, illustrating the Chinese two-tier pricing system for these important materials.

While there is evidence of worldwide activity to plan and open new mines outside of China in response to these recent price increases, bringing mines into service requires the substantial investment of time and money, on the order of hundreds of millions or even billions of dollars. The recent price spikes and volatility, together with the extraordinarily high Chinese share of production, generate uncertainty about future prices, which must be taken into account when considering investment in new mining projects. Moreover, the activities required for construction to even begin, including exploration and permitting, can take several years. For example, Ucore Rare Metals, Inc., a Canadian company that is developing an RE mining project at Bokan Mountain, Alaska, began an exploration program in 2007 and not until 2012 did it announce the hiring of a senior permitting manager who will be "working in close cooperation with the State of Alaska, the U.S. Forest Service, and associated regulators to bring Bokan into production without delay."[7]

Further causes of concern include the Chinese central government's stated policy of controlling the production of strategic materials such as the REs, antimony, and

Table 3.1
Chinese Two-Tier Pricing of Rare Earth Materials

Material	Free on Board (FOB) Prices (USD/kg)	Chinese Domestic Prices (USD/kg)
Lanthanum	66.46	18.28
Cerium	59.31	20.65
Neodymium	244.23	122.76
Praseodymium	209.62	106.94
Samarium	95.31	14.48
Dysprosium	2032.31	1085.35
Europium	3800.00	2228.38
Terbium	2973.85	1767.93

NOTE: Fourth quarter 2011.
SOURCE: Lynas Corporation Ltd., What Are Their Prices?, undated.

[7] See Ucore Rare Metals Inc., "Ucore Appoints Mine Permitting Manager for Bokan Project," Press Release, March 19, 2012.

tungsten,[8] and reports of China leveraging its position as a controlling exporter of a critical raw material in a 2010 dispute with Japan over fishing rights.[9]

The recent price spikes, volatility, and the concentration of production have also led to concern among industries dependent upon these raw materials and the products in which they are incorporated about the availability of supply. A survey of senior executives of leading global companies in the Americas, Europe, and Asia Pacific found that a majority believe supply risks will rise significantly over the next decade and that the impact will be felt throughout the supply chain. In some industries (renewable energy, automotive, and energy and utilities), the responses suggested that supply instability is already being experienced.[10] RAND verified this situation through personal discussions with leading U.S. manufacturers dependent upon raw materials of which China is a controlling producer. Their concerns included price volatility, supply instability, and a reduced competitiveness with Chinese products because their Chinese competitors have access to raw materials at lower prices. For example, one manufacturer reported seeing Chinese finished products sold at prices lower than what the U.S. manufacturer had to pay for raw materials exported from China. Another reported pressure to move its manufacturing to China in order to gain access to necessary raw materials.

China's Customers Pursue Relief at the World Trade Organization

On the same day in 2009, both the United States and the EU brought a case before the WTO regarding China's export restraints on bauxite, coke, fluorspar, magnesium, manganese, silicon metal, silicon carbide, yellow phosphorus, and zinc. Mexico brought the same case against China approximately two months later. Introducing this case, U.S. Trade Representative Ron Kirk said: "China is a leading global producer and exporter of the raw materials in question, and access to these materials is critical for U.S. industrial manufacturers. The United States is very concerned that China appears to be restricting the exports of these materials for the benefit of their domestic indus-

---

8 Ministry of Land and Resources, People's Republic of China, *National Mineral Resources Plan*, April 11, 2001; "Notice of the State Council on Listing Tungsten, Tin, Antimony and Ionic Rare Earth Minerals as National Specified Minerals Under Protective Mining," [国发] Guo Fa, No. 5, January 15, 1991. In addition to China's 90 percent antimony market share, a Chinese company purchased the only operating antimony mine in North America. See "HNC pays $29.5m for Canadian Antimony Mine," *China Daily*, September 4, 2009.

9 See Keith Bradsher, "Amid Tension, China Blocks Vital Exports to Japan," *New York Times*, September 22, 2010a. This officially undeclared embargo was reportedly also briefly extended to the United States and Europe. See, for example, Bradsher, "China Said to Widen Its Embargo of Minerals," *New York Times*, October 19, 2010b.

10 Price Waterhouse Coopers, 2011.

tries, despite strong WTO rules designed to discipline export restraints."[11] In accordance with the WTO process, a panel was established in late 2009 to examine all three complaints. The panel ruled in 2011 that China's export duties and export quotas on these materials were in violation of WTO rules. China exercised its right to appeal this ruling, and the WTO Appellate Body rejected its appeal in January 2012.[12]

Under WTO rules, China is allowed a reasonable period of time to demonstrate compliance with this ruling. However, despite some projections that this ruling against China's export restrictions might lead to an overall lessening of such restrictions, including those on REs,[13] the United States, EU, and Japan combined forces in March 2012 to bring an additional WTO case against China's export restrictions on REs, tungsten, and molybdenum. President Barack Obama announced this action at a news conference, and a statement from the U.S. Trade Representative specifically cited China's two-tier pricing: "Because China is a top global producer for these key inputs, its harmful policies artificially increase prices for the inputs outside of China while lowering prices in China." Moreover, the EU Trade Commissioner was quoted as saying, "China's restrictions on rare earths and other products violate international trade rules and must be removed. Despite a recent ruling in a separate dispute over different raw materials, China has made no attempt to remove the other export restrictions. This leaves us no choice but to challenge China's export regime again to ensure fair access for our businesses to these materials."[14]

As evidenced by the ongoing resolution of the first WTO case brought in July 2009, litigation through the WTO can take years. However, the impacts of export restrictions on U.S. manufacturers can occur much more quickly. The following chapter reviews the supply situation of tungsten as a case example for the critical raw materials of which China is the controlling producer.

---

11 For details see Office of the United States Trade Representative, "United States Files WTO Case Against China Over Export Restraints on Raw Materials," June 2009.

12 For details, see Office of the United States Trade Representative, "U.S. Trade Representative Ron Kirk Announces U.S. Victory in Challenge to China's Raw Materials Export Restraints," January 2012.

13 For example, see the quote from EU Trade Commissioner Karel De Gucht in Tom Barkley, "China Loses Trade Appeal Over Its Curb on Exports," *Wall Street Journal*, January 31, 2012.

14 For example, see CNN Wire Staff, "Obama Announces WTO Case Against China Over Rare Earths," March 13, 2012.

CHAPTER FOUR

Tungsten: Case Example of a Critical Raw Material

This chapter reviews the supply situation of tungsten, a critical raw material for which U.S. manufacturers are dependent upon imports. China is the controlling producer of tungsten, with more than 80 percent of its 2010 world mine production.[1] The situation of tungsten is typical of the critical materials and families of materials discussed in the previous chapter and, as such, provides a window for considering potential supply disruptions and possible strategies for mitigating these disruptions.

Uses and Importance of Tungsten

Because of its unique combination of high-density, high-temperature mechanical properties, high electrical conductivity, and low vapor pressure,[2] tungsten provides superior performance in many applications such as electrical lighting, high-temperature metal alloys, and wear-resistant components. Tungsten's leading use today is in cemented carbides, composite materials consisting of tungsten carbide particles in a binder, typically cobalt or nickel, that are used worldwide for drilling, cutting, and machining. These materials are critical to every industrial application that involves cutting or component wear, including mining and construction; oil and gas exploration; tools and dies; and the cutting of wood, plastics, and metals. Tungsten is thus a basic commodity underpinning the global manufacturing sector. Other important uses are in high-strength steels; high-temperature alloys; lighting filaments; electrodes; and wires, sheets, and rods used for a variety of industrial applications.[3]

---

1 U.S. Geological Survey, 2012.

2 Tungsten has the highest melting point, lowest vapor pressure, and lowest coefficient of thermal expansion of any metal. See Buffalo Tungsten Inc., "Properties of Tungsten," 2011.

3 For a detailed description of tungsten applications, see International Tungsten Industry Association (ITIA), *Tungsten*, 2008.

Tungsten Resources and Reserves

Tungsten is found throughout the world as tungsten trioxide, principally in the ores wolframite and scheelite. It exists in various types of deposits, as illustrated in Figure 4.1, with the largest deposits in Kazakhstan, China, Canada, the UK, and Russia.[4] However, China has the largest amount of reserves, which are defined as the part of the resource that is "fully geologically evaluated and legally mineable with current technology."[5] China has been the leading producer of tungsten for many years, producing at a rate far greater than any other country relative to its reserves. The distribution of worldwide tungsten reserves is shown in Figure 4.2, and a comparison of the remaining years of reserves based on current production and current consumption is shown in Figure 4.3 and Figure 4.4.[6]

The situation summarized in Figures 4.1–4.4 and shown by the tungsten component of Figure 3.1 is that tungsten is relatively abundant,[7] with substantial resources and reserves throughout the world. However, as China has increased its production of tungsten, several countries with tungsten reserves, including the United States, have ceased or reduced their production. Were these countries to resume or increase production, the world's existing reserves would appear to be sufficient for decades to come.

The Tungsten Supply Situation

The total global production of tungsten in 2010 was 68,800 metric tons of metal. China was the leading producer, producing 59,000 metric tons, or 86 percent of world production.[8] As shown in Figure 4.5, China has averaged about 75 percent of world production since 2001. U.S. data are not included in the figure because these data come from one or a few mines and are proprietary.[9]

---

4 British Geological Society, 2011, pp. 14, 16 (Figure 7). See Appendix B for details.

5 Data from U.S. Geological Survey, 2012, p. 177. Reserve definition from British Geological Society, 2011, p. 15.

6 We note that reserve and reserve-base figures are dynamic measures because resource production can become economic for a number of reasons, including higher prices and improved technology. Thus, Figure 4.3 should not be seen as predictive, but rather as a rough indicator that, at today's prices, sufficient tungsten exists in both China and the rest of the world to satisfy anticipated demands.

7 "The average abundance of tungsten in the Earth's crust is 1.25–1.5 parts per million, about the same as tin and molybdenum and half as plentiful as uranium" (British Geological Society, 2011, p. 1).

8 U.S. Geological Survey, 2012, p. 177. USGS estimates 2011 world production at 72,000 metric tons, with China producing 60,000 metric tons, or 83 percent of world production.

9 U.S. tungsten mine capacity was estimated by the U.S. International Trade Commission at 3,700 metric tons in 1989. The last published U.S. production figures in the 1980s show a reduction from around 1,000 metric tons to almost zero before data were withheld from 1988 to 1994 and production ceased from 1995 until 2007.

Figure 4.1
World Tungsten Deposits

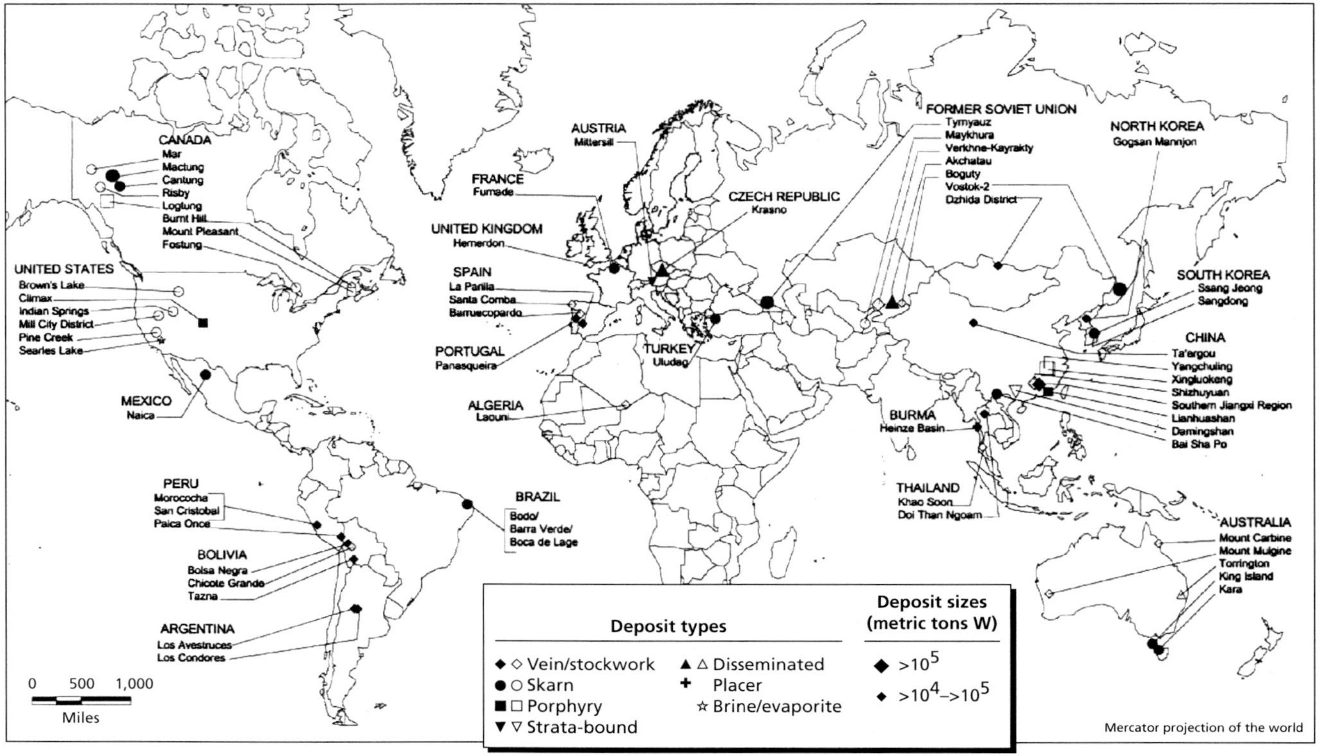

SOURCE: Antony B.T. Werner, W. David Sinclair, and Earle B. Amey, *International Strategic Mineral Issues Summary Report—Tungsten*, U.S. Geological Survey Circular 930–O, Washington, D.C.: United States Government Printing Office, 1998.

NOTE: Boundaries and country names are not necessarily authoritative. Solid symbols indicate deposits in production in 1986; unfilled symbols indicate deposits not in production in 1986.

RAND *RR133-4.1*

Figure 4.2
World Tungsten Reserves

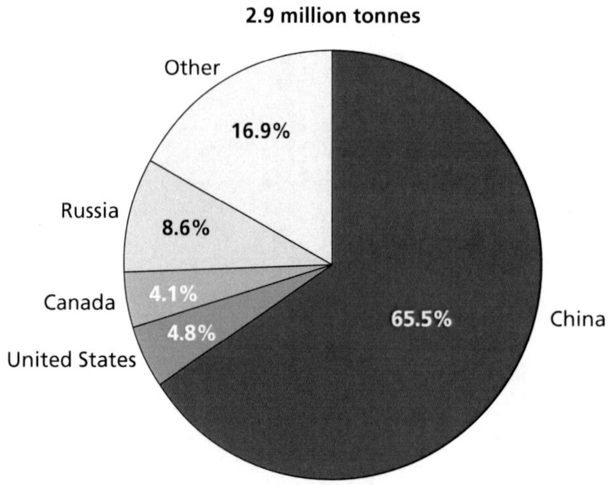

SOURCE: U.S. Geological Survey, 2011.
NOTE: 1 tonne (metric ton) = 1,000 kilograms = 2,200 pounds.
RAND *RR133-4.2*

Figure 4.3
Projected Years of Tungsten Supply Based on Production

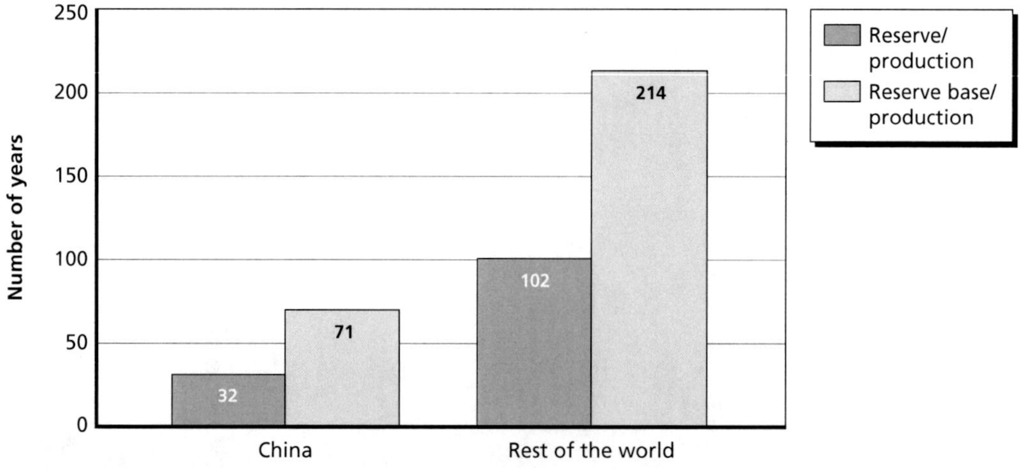

SOURCES: U.S. Geological Survey, 2009 and 2012; International Tungsten Industry Association, 2008.
NOTE: Reserve base includes the part of the resources that have a "reasonable potential for becoming economically available within planning horizons beyond those that assume proven technology and current economics" (British Geological Society, 2011).
RAND *RR133-4.3*

Figure 4.4
Projected Years of Tungsten Supply Based on Consumption

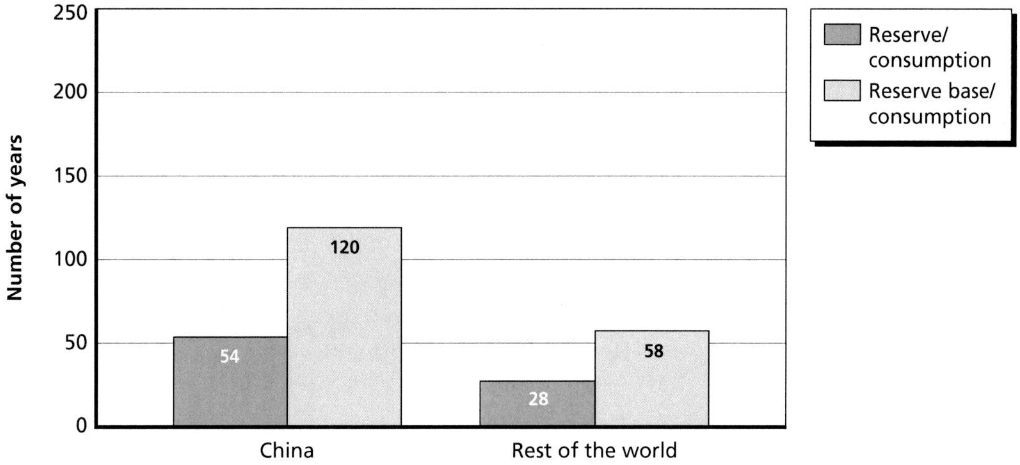

SOURCES: U.S. Geological Survey, 2009 and 2012; International Tungsten Industry Association, 2008.
NOTE: Reserve base includes the part of the resources that have a "reasonable potential for becoming economically available within planning horizons beyond those that assume proven technology and current economics" (British Geological Society, 2011).
RAND *RR133-4.4*

Figure 4.5
World Tungsten Production

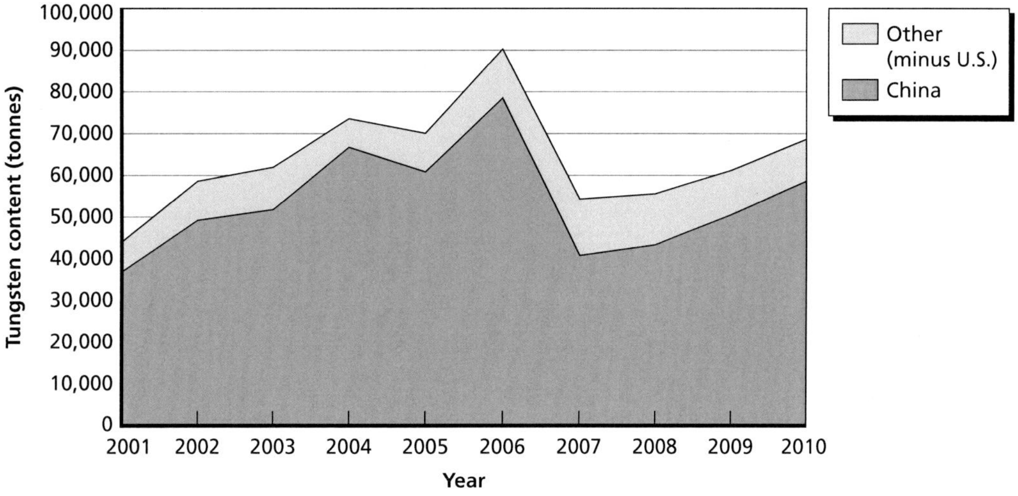

SOURCE: U.S. Geological Survey, 2003–2012.
RAND *RR133-4.5*

As China's production has increased, several countries with reserves, other than the United States, have ceased producing tungsten at some point since the 1990s: Burundi, Canada, Peru, Spain, South Korea, Uganda, Uzbekistan, and Brazil.[10] The largest remaining producer outside of China is Russia, with 3,400 metric tons. However, despite its position as the overwhelmingly dominant producer of tungsten, China is also the largest *importer* of tungsten ores and concentrates. For example, China imported over 9,000 metric tons in 2009, or a majority of the production from the rest of the world. This non-intuitive situation can be understood by examining the tungsten supply chain, shown schematically in Figure 4.6.

Tungsten is mined as wolframite or scheelite ore, which contain a low percentage of tungsten trioxide. This is concentrated to at least 65 percent tungsten trioxide through physical processing (crushing, milling, separation, and beneficiation). The concentrate is then converted, through chemical processing, into the intermediate compounds used for most applications. Perhaps the most important of these intermediate compounds is ammonium paratungstate (APT). This form of the material is the basic building block for the tungsten metal used for manufacturing,[11] and it is widely traded as a commodity. China imports tungsten ore and concentrate to supplement its domestic production, processes these into APT and other intermediates, then exports them as well as final products, such as steel and cemented carbides. Thus, China is not only the controlling producer of tungsten ore and concentrate—it is also the controlling producer of the most important intermediate tungsten compound, APT.

With only one producing mine, the United States is dependent on imports, material obtained from the NDS, and secondary production from scrap and waste[12] for most of its tungsten ore and concentrate and intermediate compounds, including APT, with most of the latter coming from China. The flow of these materials between the United States, China, and the rest of the world in 2010 is illustrated in Figure 4.7, in which ore and concentrate flows are shown in green, intermediate compounds in blue, and metal in red.

---

[10] U.S. Geological Survey, *Minerals Yearbook: Vol. I–Metals and Minerals*, Pittsburgh, Penn.: U.S. Government Printing Office, 1997, p. 16.; 2001, p. 17; 2005, p. 19; 2010, p. 22.

[11] As shown in the figure, the exception is steel manufacturing, for which ferrotungsten and ferrosilicon tungsten are the intermediate compounds.

[12] ITIA estimates that 34 percent of global demand for tungsten ore and concentrate and intermediate products is satisfied by scrap and waste, with 24 percent coming from used parts (scrap) and 10 percent from processing (waste). See British Geological Society, 2011, p. 55. These two sources have very different ramifications for domestic tungsten supply, since scrap derived from parts that were previously imported can reduce current import dependence, while waste from the processing of imported tungsten merely provides more efficient use of current imports.

Figure 4.6
Schematic Representation of the Tungsten Supply Chain

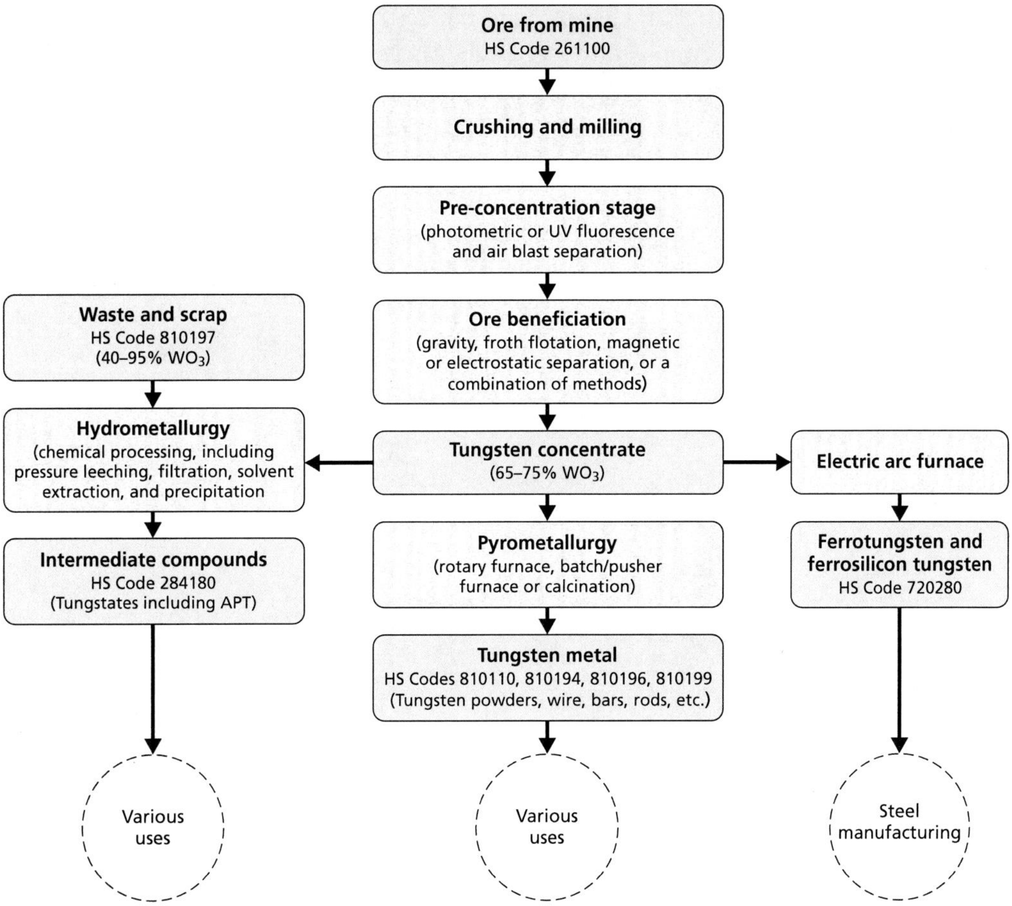

SOURCES: British Geological Society, 2011; United Nations Comtrade, *Trade Statistics Database*, undated.
NOTE: Blue designates forms of tungsten, while gray designates processing steps. HS codes are the codes of the Harmonized Tariff System, a commodity coding system adopted by most nations of the world and used in the UN Comtrade database.
RAND *RR133-4.6*

The material flows shown in Figure 4.7 can be represented by the following supply-demand balance equation:[13]

$$(\text{Production} + \text{Stockpile Reduction}) + (\text{Imports} - \text{Exports}) = \text{Consumption}$$

[13] The production figure includes secondary production from scrap and waste. Imports and exports also include scrap and waste.

where the sets of parentheses on the left-hand side of the equation designate the sources of a material produced or resident inside a country and the increase or decrease in that material due to trade, respectively. Figure 4.7 shows that both the United States and China import much more tungsten ore and concentrate than they export, while the rest of the world exports much more ore and concentrate than it imports. For intermediate products, the situation is reversed, with China exporting much more than it imports and the rest of the world importing much more than it exports, while the United States is a net importer by a smaller margin. Since China is the overwhelmingly dominant producer of the tungsten ore and concentrate from which intermediate tungsten products are produced (see Figure 4.6), the result of the above equation demonstrates the strong dependence of both the United States and the rest of the world on Chinese exports of intermediate tungsten products such as APT.[14] In the event of a

Figure 4.7
Tungsten Raw Materials Supply Network

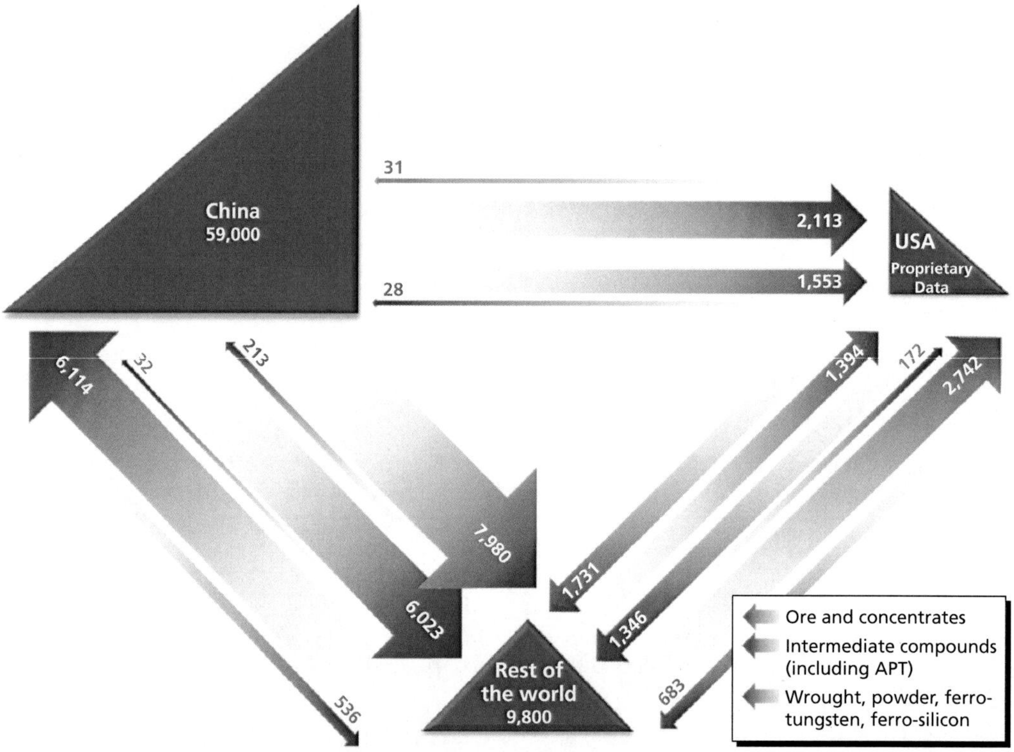

SOURCES: U.S. Geological Survey; United Nations Comtrade, undated.
NOTE: Units are metric tons (tonnes). Figures below country names denote domestic production. U.S. data is proprietary and not disclosed by the USGS.
RAND *RR133-4.7*

[14] This dependence can be reduced by material from stockpiles and secondary production from waste and scrap.

disruption in these exports, it would be difficult for the United States or the rest of the world to provide substitute material because of the time required (at least several years, as noted previously) to develop projects to mine new ore or process ore and concentrates into intermediate products.

As shown in Figure 4.8, Chinese domestic consumption of tungsten (principally metal and intermediate products by its manufacturing sector) has been increasing in recent years, while its exports of tungsten (principally metal and intermediate products) have been flat or decreasing. As a result, analysts inside and outside of China foresee a tight supply situation over the next several years. For example, a Chinese metal and mining industry consulting firm, Antaike, projected that Chinese domestic consumption would rise at a more rapid rate than its production through 2015.[15] Ormonde Mining Plc, a mineral resource company listed in Ireland, which is carrying out exploration and developing tungsten mining projects in Spain, estimated a global market deficit, excluding China and Russia, of 14,500 metric tons in 2013, based on its projected reduction in imports from China of 7,500 metric tons between 2008 and 2013.[16]

Figure 4.8
Chinese Domestic Consumption and Exports of Tungsten

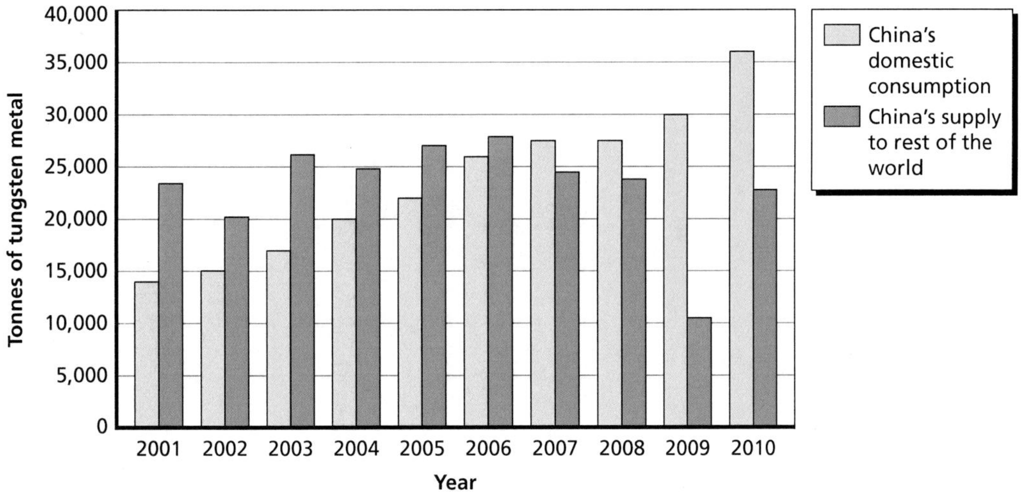

SOURCE: Ormonde Mining Plc, 2010.
RAND *RR133-4.8*

[15] Xu Aihua and Li Bingxin, "Analysis on China's Tungsten Industry in 2010–2011," Beijing Antaike Information Development Company Ltd., briefing presented at MB 26th Ferro-Alloys Conference, Germany, November 2010.

[16] Ormonde Mining Plc, *Tungsten Market Overview*, 2010. China has been reducing export quotas since 2006. For example, see Somerley Limited, *Market Report on Tungsten, Fluorspar, Bismuth and Copper*, August 2011, p. 16. These figures do not include the "foreign investment quota," a much smaller number that, before 2010, was reported separately. For details, see U.S. Geological Survey, *Minerals Yearbook*, 2010.

Figure 4.9 shows the response of the world APT price to tight supplies. The price of APT more than doubled from early 2010 to mid-2011, rising to a historic high over four times its early 2000s level.[17] This price spike has led to renewed interest in resuming production at existing mines and opening new mines, for example:[18]

- North American Tungsten resumed production at its Cantung mine in Canada's Western Territories in October 2010
- Ormonde Mining Plc is planning to commission its Barruecopardo mine in western Spain in third quarter 2013
- Playfair Mining (several properties in Canada), Wolf Minerals (Hemerdon Ball project in the UK), and Woulfe Mining (Sandong project in South Korea) are developing tungsten mining projects.

However, as noted previously, the price uncertainty resulting from China's market control is a potential barrier to financing for such projects.

Figure 4.9
Tungsten Price Increases in 2010 and 2011

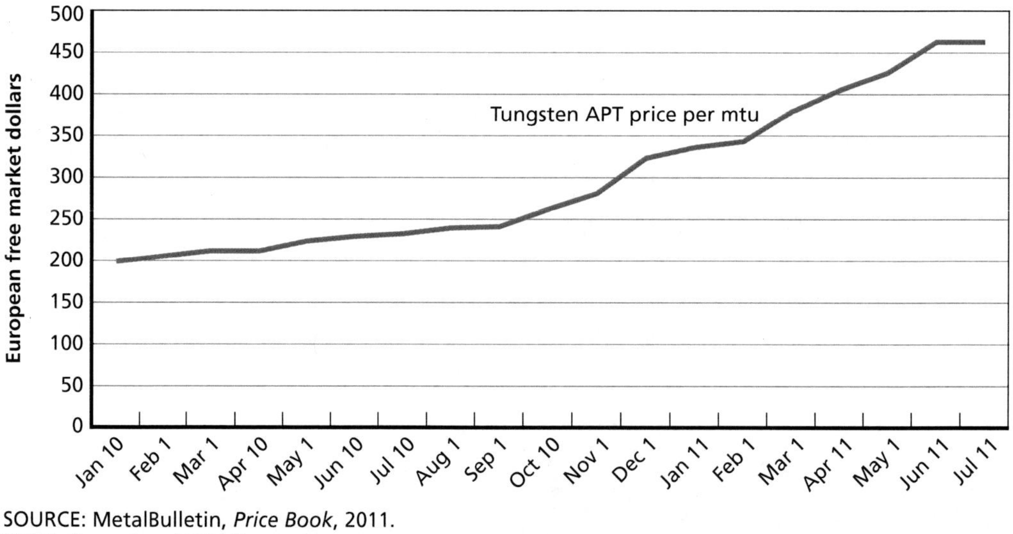

SOURCE: MetalBulletin, *Price Book*, 2011.
NOTE: One mtu = 7.93 kilograms.
RAND *RR133-4.9*

[17] APT price was relatively stable between July 2011 and May 2012, when it dropped slightly below $400/metric ton unit (mtu), then recovered to $400/mtu, where it remained from mid-June to mid-August 2012. See Metal-Pages, "Metal Prices–Tungsten," 2012.

[18] Michael Montgomery, "Tungsten Production Outside of China," *Tungsten Investing News*, June 29, 2011.

The U.S. response to tight tungsten supplies and high prices has been a remarkable increase in secondary production from scrap and waste, rising in 2011 to an estimated level of 55 percent of apparent consumption,[19] which reduced U.S. import dependence from over 60 percent in recent years to less than 40 percent in 2011, as shown in Figure 4.10. This level of secondary production is considerably higher than recent or historical levels.[20] However, a detailed analysis of the source of this increase is required to determine whether it is sustainable and how much further secondary production might be increased in the event of additional supply restrictions or price surges. If the observed increase in secondary production has been obtained by recycling waste that has accumulated over time, then it is accessing a finite resource that will eventually be depleted, like a stockpile. On the other hand, if the observed increase in secondary production reflects an increase in the recycling of current waste, then it is sustainable, but the question arises as to what level of recycling can be achieved over the long term.

Figure 4.10
U.S. Tungsten Production and Dependence on Imports

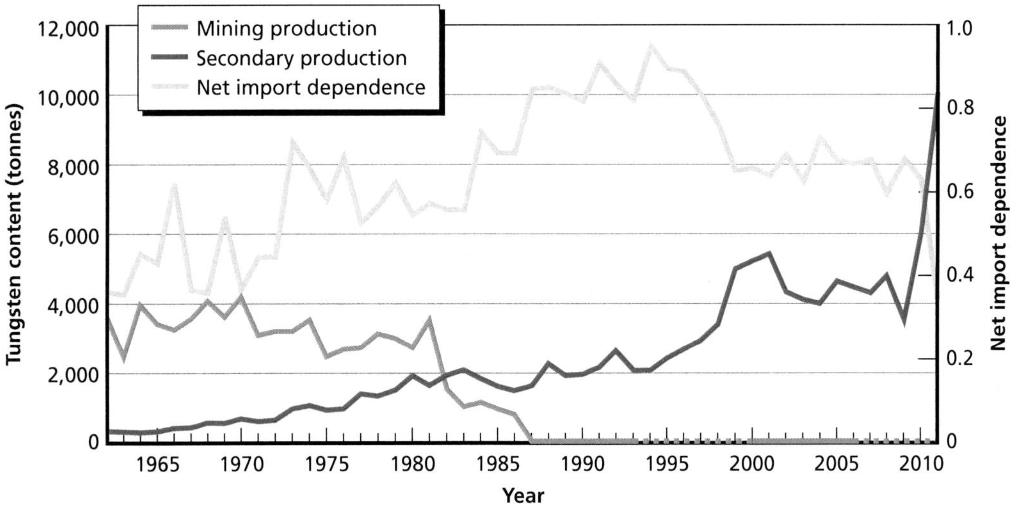

SOURCES: Thomas D. Kelly and Grecia R. Matos, *Historical Statistics for Mineral and Material Commodities in the United States*, U.S. Geological Survey, Data Series 140, 2011; U.S. Geological Survey, 1997–2012.
NOTE: Mining and secondary production are shown on the left-hand axis; net import dependence on the right.
RAND *RR133-4.10*

---

[19] Secondary production was estimated by the USGS as 10,000 metric tons in 2011, and apparent consumption was estimated at 18,200 metric tons (U.S. Geological Survey, 2012, p. 177).

[20] A detailed analysis of U.S. tungsten materials flow in 2000 provided an estimate of secondary production as 42.6 percent of apparent consumption, taking into account the sources of both old (from scrapped products) and new (from fabrication of products) waste, as well as imports. See Kim B. Shedd, *Tungsten Recycling in the United States in 2000*, U.S. Geological Survey, Open-File Report 2005-1028, Pittsburgh, Penn.: U.S. Government Printing Office, 2005.

Numerous events in China, such as the tightening of environmental or safety standards,[21] the closing of illegal mines, internal strife, or a natural disaster,[22] could lead to a disruption of production and a further tightening of tungsten supply. Also, based on China's stated policies and the two-tier pricing structure described previously, the question arises as to whether China's domestic manufacturers would receive preferential access if supply were limited. Such a policy would further exacerbate the supply situation for non-Chinese manufacturers dependent on raw and semi-finished tungsten materials.

Potential Impacts of the Tungsten Supply Situation

As shown in the previous section, manufacturers in the United States and other countries are dependent on Chinese exports of intermediate tungsten compounds and are currently faced with historically high prices for these materials. Moreover, a tight supply is foreseen over the next several years. Adding to this the uncertainties associated with Chinese production and export policies and domestic consumption as well as the pervasive use throughout the U.S. manufacturing sector of tungsten carbide-based cutting tools, the potential exists for serious impacts on U.S. manufacturing. These impacts would have both short-term and long-term consequences. The U.S. science and technology base that supports the manufacturing of cemented carbides, tungsten mill products, and steels and alloys containing tungsten was built on, and therefore depends on, the presence of U.S. manufacturers producing these products from raw and semi-finished tungsten. Prolonged disruption in the supply of raw and semi-finished tungsten required by these manufacturers could, in turn, put the science and technology base in jeopardy, which would further reduce U.S. innovation capability and competitiveness in the development of new, higher-performance products in areas such as cutting tools and high-temperature metals and alloys.[23]

Our discussions with U.S. manufacturers suggest that they are already taking steps toward reducing the intensity of tungsten in their products, to the extent that this can be done without reducing performance, and they are considering and researching alternative materials and product designs. Over the long term, such efforts, along with research and development into improved methods of processing, recovery, and recycling, have great potential. However, any resolution of the tungsten supply situa-

[21] For such actions on antimony mining, see U.S. Geological Survey, 2012, p. 19.

[22] More than 60 percent of China's tungsten reserves are in three neighboring provinces. British Geological Society, 2011, p. 15.

[23] For a discussion of how China's control of rare earth production and manufacturing has led to extensive reduction in the quality and quantity of the U.S. science and technology base for rare earth materials see, for example, Gschneider, Jr., 2011.

tion over the next several years will have to come from measures to diversify supply, as well as efforts to ensure that the current controlling producer, China, abides by market rules, which is the objective of the current actions at the WTO, described earlier.

CHAPTER FIVE

Conclusions and Response Options

The data and analyses presented in this report suggest that issues with the supply of minerals are less about the minerals themselves and more about where the raw and semi-finished materials that underpin the world's economies are produced and processed. One clear conclusion is that producers who command a large market share of a mineral's supply can distort mineral commodity markets through production controls and export restrictions. Thus, it is the concentration of supply and, in particular, its concentration among producing countries that either have weak governance or that control production at the governmental level, or both, that can increase the potential for supply disruptions.

While much has been written recently about RE elements, we argue that these materials are not the only sources of concern. In Chapter Two, we identify 14 different materials for which production is concentrated in countries with weak governance, as defined by low WGI percentiles. China is the controlling producer of 11 of these critical raw materials. As described in Chapters Three and Four, China's strategic material policies, including efforts to control the production outside China of materials such as antimony and REs, of which it is already an overwhelmingly controlling producer, as well as its imposition of production quotas and export restrictions, have contributed to large price increases, some price volatility, tight markets, and uncertainty that can hinder the financing of new mining projects. China's policies contrast with those of other countries with high market shares, such as Chile (with 53 percent of rhenium) and Australia (with 51 percent of zirconium), which do not implement export restrictions,[1] instead allowing market forces to largely determine supply and demand of the minerals they produce. While prices of these countries' commodities could also increase or become volatile, their governments' actions are not likely to be a significant contributing factor.

Market distortions for raw and semi-finished materials can be felt strongly in the manufacturing sector, where these materials are a critical input. As a result, the United States, as well as the EU, Japan, and Mexico, have pursued actions against China's

---

[1] See Kim, 2010, pp. 26 and 33.

export policies at the WTO. However, the WTO follows an exacting legal process that typically takes years to resolve a dispute. For example, a case brought against China by the United States, EU, and Mexico in 2009 is still in its final stages of resolution. In contrast, the impacts on manufacturers of price increases or supply reductions of necessary input materials are felt more promptly. This suggests the need for two types of actions: (1) those that can increase resiliency to supply disruptions or market distortions and (2) those that can provide early warning of developing problems concerning the concentration of production.

Increasing Resiliency to Supply Disruptions or Market Distortions

The first line of defense against supply disruption or market distortion is to reduce the magnitude of the potential problem by preventing any controlling producer from further increasing its market share of a material. As mentioned in Chapter Three, while China already controls 90 percent of worldwide antimony production, a Chinese company purchased the only operating antimony mine in North America (in Canada), further increasing China's control of the antimony market. However, China's attempt to acquire a controlling interest in Lynas Corporation, the owner of the Mount Weld RE mining project in Australia, which, once in operation, would have increased China's 98 percent market share, was blocked by Australia's Foreign Investment Review Board.[2]

While the actions described above were taken by individual countries, coordination among multiple countries dependent upon a controlling producer for raw or semifinished materials will sometimes be necessary to limit the potential for market distortion or supply disruption. For example, as shown in Chapter Four, in addition to being the controlling producer, China is also the world's largest importer of tungsten ore and concentrate, and the controlling processor of this ore and concentrate into intermediate products. A coordinated effort to increase processing in other countries would reduce the level of China's control over the tungsten supply chain. Where the ore and concentrate is processed is important because the processing country has the ability to manipulate the supply of the intermediate products and metals critical to manufacturing. Although such manipulation may be restricted by WTO rules, actions to enforce these rules, as discussed earlier, typically take years to resolve. For example, China also controls both the production and processing of REs. A recent proposal to send RE ore from the only operating U.S. RE mine to China for processing has become controversial for this reason.[3]

---

2 See Reuters, "China Fails in Another Bid for Resources Firm," *The Sydney Morning Herald*, September 29, 2009.

3 This resulted from Molycorp, owner of the Mountain Pass, California, mine, seeking to acquire Toronto-based Neo Material Technologies, which operates RE processing plants in China. For example, see Julie Gordon, "DEAL TALK-Molycorp, Neo Material Deal a Rare Earth Game Changer," *Reuters*, March 11, 2012.

Diversifying Production

Since the main source of the supply problems discussed here is the concentration of production, the most effective action that can be taken to increase resiliency would be to encourage diversified production, i.e., the operation of mines in several different countries. Indeed, such diversification is already beginning to take place, as discussed in Chapters Three and Four. However, the uncertainty created by a highly concentrated market is a barrier that must be overcome by actions at the local, national, regional, and global levels to create a favorable and sustainable climate for the investments and time needed to bring diversified supplies into place. Coordinated actions by importing countries may be effective here as well. Other areas where coordination is possible include the filling of stockpiles and the establishment of agreements about sharing limited resources in the event of supply disruptions.

Long-Term Actions to Increase Resiliency

Over the long term, actions to increase resiliency may include the development of new methods of extraction, processing, and manufacturing that promote the efficient use of materials, as well as the increased recovery of materials from waste and scrap (secondary production). These actions, as well as the research and development of alternative materials[4] and new product designs to reduce the demand for limited materials, are already being pursued.

Foresight of Developing Problems

Many organizations collect and report data on the production, processing, and trade of minerals. For example, we were able to develop a comprehensive picture of the tungsten supply situation using data from the USGS, the British Geological Society, the ITIA, and the UN's Comtrade database. However, early warning of a developing problem related to the control of a mineral market by one or a few producing countries requires an understanding of the motivation and intent of producing countries and companies, as well as the tracking and monitoring of international agreements and activities among both producing and consuming countries.

How might we recognize a developing pattern, such as an increasing concentration of production, increasing export restrictions, two-tier pricing, price spikes, or price volatility, before it creates harmful market distortions? How can we tell whether a trend is part of the natural development of a producing country from an economy dependent on the export of raw and semi-finished materials to one that produces and

[4] For example, the U.S. Department of Energy's Rare Earth Alternatives in Critical Technologies (REACT) program is working to develop substitutes to RE elements for electric vehicle motors and wind generators. See Alexa McClanahan, "ARPA-E Awards 156 Million for Groundbreaking Energy Research Projects," October 31, 2011.

exports more value-added products? Here, international coordination and the benchmarking of market activity with diversified commodity markets can provide a guide. For example, the U.S. Department of Justice's criterion for a transaction that is "presumed likely to enhance market power in a highly concentrated market" is a change of .02 in the HHI discussed in Chapter Two. Consider a hypothetical case in which each of five countries has a 20 percent market share, which gives an HHI of .2, a moderately concentrated market by our criteria. If one of these countries acquired an additional 10 percent market share from one of the others, then the HHI would increase from .20 to .22, which would meet the Department of Justice threshold for enhancing market power. When such situations occur, international coordination and cooperation could potentially prevent them from reaching the level of concern characterized by the recent actions against China brought before the WTO by the United States, the EU, and Japan. The goal of such coordination and cooperation should be to smooth market distortions while allowing for the natural economic development of producing countries.

APPENDIX A

Top Three Producers of the 41 EC Critical Raw Materials

Table A.1 lists the 2010 market shares of the top three producers of the 41 critical raw materials defined by the EC's Ad-hoc Working Group on defining raw materials. Figures appearing in red denote a market share of greater than 50 percent.[1]

Table A.1
Top Three Producers of the 41 EC Critical Raw Materials

Mineral	Major Producer	Share (%)
Aluminum	China	39.7
	Russia	9.7
	Canada	7.2
Antimony	China	89.8
	Bolivia	3.0
	Russia	1.8
	South Africa	1.8
Barites	China	51.0
	India	14.0
	United States	8.4
Bauxite	Australia	32.7
	China	21.1
	Brazil	13.4
Bentonite	United States	43.6
	Turkey	11.3
	Greece	8.0

[1] U.S. Geological Survey, 2012.

Table A.1—Continued

Mineral	Major Producer	Share (%)
Beryllium	United States	87.8
	China	10.7
	Mozambique	1.0
Boron[a]	Turkey	49.0
	Argentina	14.7
	Chile	12.4
Chromium	South Africa	46.0
	Kazakhstan	16.2
	India	16.0
Clays	United States	25.6
	Uzbekistan	11.7
	Germany	10.3
Cobalt	Congo	52.9
	China	7.2
	Russia	6.9
Copper	Chile	34.0
	Peru	7.9
	China	7.5
Diatomite	United States	32.7
	China	22.0
	Denmark	12.4
Feldspar	Turkey	24.3
	Italy	22.8
	China	10.2
Fluorspar	China	54.9
	Mexico	17.8
	Mongolia	7.0
Gallium[b]	China	59.5
	Ukraine	15.5
	Kazakhstan	13.1

Table A.1—Continued

Mineral	Major Producer	Share (%)
Germanium	China	67.8
	Russia	4.2
	United States	2.5
Graphite	China	64.9
	India	15.1
	Brazil	8.2
Gypsum	China	31.9
	Iran	8.8
	Spain	7.8
Indium	China	55.8
	Japan	11.5
	Republic of Korea	11.5
Iron (Ore)	China	41.3
	Australia	16.7
	Brazil	14.3
Lime	China	61.1
	United States	5.9
	India	4.5
Lithium[c]	Chile	37.4
	Australia	33.0
	China	14.0
Magnesite[d]	China	70.1
	Russia	6.0
	Turkey	5.0
Magnesium	China	86.4
	Russia	4.9
	Israel	3.3
Manganese	Australia	22.3
	South Africa	20.9
	China	18.7

Table A.1—Continued

Mineral	Major Producer	Share (%)
Molybdenum	China	38.7
	United States	24.5
	Chile	15.4
Nickel	Russia	16.9
	Indonesia	14.6
	Philippines	10.9
Niobium	Brazil	92.2
	Canada	7.0
Perlite	Greece	29.9
	United States	24.8
	Turkey	13.8
Platinum Group Metals	South Africa	58.9
	Russia	27.9
	Zimbabwe	4.0
Rare Earths	China	97.2
	India	2.1
	Brazil	0.2
Rhenium	Chile	53.0
	United States	12.9
	Peru	10.6
Silica Sand/Gravel	United States	24.7
	Italy	16.4
	Germany	5.8
Silver	Mexico	19.1
	Peru	15.8
	China	15.2
Talc	China	27.7
	Republic of Korea	9.8
	India	8.8

Table A.1—Continued

Mineral	Major Producer	Share (%)
Tantalum[e]	Brazil	26.4
	Mozambique	17.6
	Rwanda	16.2
Tellurium[f]	Japan	63.5
	Canada	25.4
	Peru	11.1
Titanium	Australia	23.7
	South Africa	17.4
	Canada	10.7
Tungsten[g]	China	85.8
	Russia	4.1
	Portugal	1.7
	Bolivia	1.7
Vanadium[h]	China	38.6
	South Africa	33.3
	Russia	26.3
Zinc	China	30.8
	Australia	12.3
	Peru	12.3

[a] U.S. figures withheld.
[b] 2009 figure, International Organizing Committee for the World Mining Congresses, 2011.
[c] U.S. figures withheld.
[d] U.S. figures withheld.
[e] Excludes tantalum obtained from tin slags.
[f] 2009 figure, International Organizing Committee for the World Mining Congresses, 2011.
[g] U.S. figures withheld.
[h] U.S. figures withheld.

APPENDIX B

The World's Largest Tungsten Deposits

The world's largest deposits of tungsten (at least 100,000 metric tons of metal) are found in Kazakhstan, Canada, China, the UK, Russia, and Australia, as shown in Table B.1.

Table B.1
The World's Largest Tungsten Deposits

Deposit name (Location)	Country	Estimated Tungsten Content (thousands of metric tons of metal)
Verkhne-Kayrakty (Dzhezkazgan Oblast)	Kazakhstan	872
Mactung (Yukon & Northwest Territories)	Canada	617
Shizuyuan (Hunan)	China	502
Hemerdon (SW England)	UK	309
Trynyauz (Kabardino-Balkaria)	Russia	244
Northern Dancer (Yukon)	Canada	168
Yangchuling (Janxi)	China	160
Xingluokeng/Xianglushan (Fujian)	China	144
O'Callaghan's (Western Australia)	Australia	135
Damingshan (Guangxi)	China	116
Vostok-2 (Primorskye)	Russia	102
Ta'ergou (Gansu)	China	100
Total		3,469

SOURCE: British Geological Society, 2011, p. 15.

Bibliography

Barkley, Tom, "China Loses Trade Appeal Over Its Curb on Exports," *Wall Street Journal*, January 31, 2012.

Bradsher, Keith, "Amid Tension, China Blocks Vital Exports to Japan," *New York Times*, September 22, 2010a. As of June 6, 2012:
http://www.nytimes.com/2010/09/23/business/global/23rare.html?pagewanted=all.

———, "China Said to Widen Its Embargo of Minerals," *New York Times*, October 19, 2010b. As of June 6, 2012:
http://www.nytimes.com/2010/10/20/business/global/20rare.html?pagewanted=all.

British Geological Society, *Tungsten*, 2011.

Buffalo Tungsten Inc., "Properties of Tungsten," 2011. As of June 6, 2012:
http://www.buffalotungsten.com/html/properties.html

Committee on Critical Mineral Impacts of the U.S. Economy, Committee on Earth Resources, and the National Research Council, *Minerals, Critical Minerals, and the U.S. Economy*, Washington, D.C.: National Academies Press, 2008, p. 165.

CNN Wire Staff, "Obama Announces WTO Case Against China Over Rare Earths," March 13, 2012. As of June 6, 2012:
http://www.cnn.com/2012/03/13/world/asia/china-rare-earths-case/index.html

European Commission, "Critical Raw Materials for the EU," *Report of the Ad-hoc Working Group on defining raw materials*, June 2010, p. 6.

Goonan, Thomas G., *Rare Earth Elements–End Use and Recyclability*, U.S. Geological Survey, Pittsburgh, Penn.: U.S. Government Printing Office, 2011.

Gordon, Julie, "DEAL TALK-Molycorp, Neo Material Deal a Rare Earth Game Changer," *Reuters*, March 11, 2012. As of November 5, 2012:
http://www.reuters.com/article/2012/03/11/neomaterial-molycorp-idUSL2E8E9AZW20120311.

Gshneider, K. A., Jr., "The Rare Earth Crisis—The Supply/Demand Situation for 2010–2015," *Material Matters*, Vol. 6, No. 2, 2011, p. 32.

"Herfindahl-Hirschman Index," U.S. Department of Justice, undated. As of November 5, 2012:
http://www.justice.gov/atr/public/testimony/hhi.htm

Hirschman, Albert O., "The Paternity of an Index," *American Economic Review*, Vol. 54, No. 5, September 1964, p. 761.

"HNC pays $29.5m for Canadian Antimony Mine," *China Daily*, September 4, 2009. As of June 6, 2012:
http://www.chinadaily.com.cn/bizchina/2009-09/04/content_8654294.htm

International Organizing Committee for the World Mining Congresses, *World Mining Data*, Vol. 26, 2011.

International Tungsten Industry Association (ITIA), *Tungsten*, 2008.

Kaufman, Daniel, Aart Kraay, and Massimo Mastruzzi, *The Worldwide Governance Indicators: Methodology and Analytical Issues*, World Bank Policy Research Working Paper 5430, September 2010.

Kelly, Thomas D., and Grecia R. Matos, *Historical Statistics for Mineral and Material Commodities in the United States*, U.S. Geological Survey, Data Series 140, 2011.

Kim, Jeonghoi, "Recent Trends in Export Restrictions," *OECD Trade Policy Papers*, No. 101, Paris: OECD Publishing, 2010. As of June 6, 2012:
http://dx.doi.org/10.1787/5kmbjx63sl27-en

Korinek, Jane, and Jeonghoi Kim, "Export Restrictions on Strategic Raw Materials and Their Impact on Trade and the Global Supply," *OECD Trade Policy Papers*, No. 95, Paris: OECD Publishing, 2010.

Lynas Corporation Ltd., *What Are Their Prices?* As of June 6, 2012:
http://www.lynascorp.com/page.asp?category_id=1&page_id=25

McClanahan, Alexa, "ARPA-E Awards 156 Million for Groundbreaking Energy Research Projects," October 31, 2011. As of June 6, 2012:
http://energy.gov/articles/arpa-e-awards-156-million-groundbreaking-energy-research-projects

MetalBulletin, *Price Book,* 2011. As of June 6, 2012:
http://www.metalbulletin.com/

Metal-Pages, "Metal Prices–Tungsten," 2012. As of August 29, 2012:
http://www.metal-pages.com/metalprices/tungsten

Ministry of Land and Resources, People's Republic of China, *National Mineral Resources Plan*, April 11, 2001.

Montgomery, Michael, "Tungsten Price Pushes to Historic Highs," *Tungsten Investing News*, February 23, 2011a. As of August 26, 2012:
http://tungsteninvestingnews.com/895-tungsten-price-pushes-to-historic-highs.html

———, "Tungsten Production Outside of China," *Tungsten Investing News*, June 29, 2011b. As of November 5, 2012:
http://tungsteninvestingnews.com/1173-tungsten-production-outside-of-china.html.

"Notice of the State Council on Listing Tungsten, Tin, Antimony and Ionic Rare Earth Minerals as National Specified Minerals Under Protective Mining," [国发] Guo Fa, No. 5, January 15, 1991.

Office of the United States Trade Representative, "United States Files WTO Case Against China Over Export Restraints on Raw Materials," June 2009. As of June 6, 2012:
http://www.ustr.gov/about-us/press-office/press-releases/2009/june/
united-states-files-wto-case-against-china-over-expor

———, "U.S. Trade Representative Ron Kirk Announces U.S. Victory in Challenge to China's Raw Materials Export Restraints," January 2012. As of June 6, 2012:
http://www.ustr.gov/about-us/press-office/press-releases/2012/january/
us-trade-representative-ron-kirk-announces-us-vict

Ormonde Mining Plc, *Tungsten Market Overview*, 2010.

Pitfield, Peter, and Teresa Brown, *Tungsten Profile*, British Geological Survey, January 2011.

Price Waterhouse Coopers, *Minerals and Metals Scarcity in Manufacturing: The Ticking Timebomb: Sustainable Materials Management*, December 2011. As of June 6, 2012:
http://www.pwc.com/en_GX/gx/sustainability/research-insights/assets/impact-of-minerals-metals-scarcity-on-business.pdf

Reuters, "China Fails in Another Bid for Resources Firm," *The Sydney Morning Herald*, September 29, 2009. As of June 6, 2012:
http://www.smh.com.au/business/china-fails-in-another-bid-for-resources-firm-20090924-g417.html

Shedd, Kim B., *Tungsten Recycling in the United States in 2000*, U.S. Geological Survey, Open-File Report 2005-1028, Pittsburgh, Penn.: U.S. Government Printing Office, 2005. As of November 5, 2012:
http://pubs.usgs.gov/of/2005/1028/2005-1028.pdf

Somerley Limited, *Market Report on Tungsten, Fluorspar, Bismuth and Copper*, August 2011, p. 16. As of June 6, 2012:
http://www.masangroup.com/static/uploads/block/somerly-report-en-6.pdf

Strategic Metal Investments, Ltd., *China's Growing Role in the Production and Supply of Minor Metals: Part II*, May 10, 2010. As of June 6, 2012:
http://www.strategic-metal.com/index.php/news/content/
Chinas_growing_role_production_supply_minor_metals_partII

Thomason, James S., Robert J. Atwell, Ylli Bajraktari, James P. Bell, D. Sean Barnett, Nicholas S.J. Karvonides, Michael F. Niles, and Eleanor L. Schwartz, *From National Defense Stockpile (NDS) to Strategic Materials Security Program (SMSP) Vol. I: Evidence and Analytic Support*, Alexandria, Va.: Institute for Defense Analyses, 2010, pp. 10–11. As of June 5, 2012:
http://www.dtic.mil/cgi-bin/GetTRDoc?AD=ADA527258

Ucore Rare Metals Inc., "Ucore Appoints Mine Permitting Manager for Bokan Project," Press Release, March 19, 2012. As of June 6, 2012:
http://ucore.com/ucore-appoints-mine-permitting-manager-for-bokan-project

United Nations Comtrade, *Trade Statistics Database*. As of June 6, 2012:
http://comtrade.un.org/db/

United States Antimony Corporation, home page, 2012. As of December 19, 2012:
http://www.usantimony.com/

U.S. Department of Energy, *Critical Materials Strategy*, December 2011, p. 4. As of June 6, 2012:
http://energy.gov/sites/prod/files/DOE_CMS2011_FINAL_Full.pdf

U.S. Geological Survey, *Minerals Yearbook: Vol. I–Metals and Minerals*, Pittsburgh, Penn.: U.S. Government Printing Office, 1994–2010. As of June 5, 2012:
http://minerals.usgs.gov/minerals/pubs/commodity/myb/

———, *Minerals Commodity Summaries*, Pittsburgh, Penn.: U.S. Government Printing Office, 1996–2012. As of June 5, 2012:
http://minerals.usgs.gov/minerals/pubs/mcs/2012/mcs2012.pdf

Werner, Antony B.T., W. David Sinclair, and Earle B. Amey, *International Strategic Mineral Issues Summary Report—Tungsten*, U.S. Geological Survey Circular 930–O, Washington, D.C.: United States Government Printing Office, 1998.

The World Bank, *Worldwide Governance Indicators*, 2012. As of November 6, 2012:
http://info.worldbank.org/governance/wgi/index.asp

World Trade Organization, *China–Measures Related to the Exportation of Various Raw Materials*, Dispute Settlement: DS394, February 22, 2012a. As of June 5, 2012: http://www.wto.org/english/tratop_e/dispu_e/cases_e/ds394_e.htm

———, *China—Measures Related to the Exportation of Rare Earths, Tungsten and Molybdenum*, Dispute Settlement: DS431, September 24, 2012b. As of November 6, 2012: http://www.wto.org/english/tratop_e/dispu_e/cases_e/ds431_e.htm

———, *China—Measures Related to the Exportation of Rare Earths, Tungsten and Molybdenum*, Dispute Settlement: DS432, September 24, 2012c. As of November 6, 2012: http://www.wto.org/english/tratop_e/dispu_e/cases_e/ds432_e.htm

———, *China—Measures Related to the Exportation of Rare Earths, Tungsten and Molybdenum*, Dispute Settlement: DS433, September 24, 2012d. As of November 6, 2012: http://www.wto.org/english/tratop_e/dispu_e/cases_e/ds433_e.htm

Xu Aihua and Li Bingxin, "Analysis on China's Tungsten Industry in 2010–2011," Beijing Antaike Information Development Company Ltd., briefing presented at MB 26th Ferro-Alloys Conference, Germany, November 2010.